Raking the Winter Leaves

GARY MARGOLIS

Raking the Winter Leaves

NEW & SELECTED POEMS

Bauhan Publishing
Peterborough · New Hampshire
2013

Library of Congress Cataloging-in-Publication Data

Margolis, Gary.
[Poems. Selections]
Raking the Winter Leaves : new and selected poems / Gary Margolis.
    pages cm
ISBN 978-0-87233-171-6 (alk. paper)
I. Title.
PS3563.A6495A6 2013
811'.54--dc23

2013038014

Also by Gary Margolis

The Day We Still Stand Here

Falling Awake

Fire in the Orchard

Below the Falls

Seeing the Songs: A Poet's Journey to the Shamans in Ecuador

Photo of the author by Wendy Lynch

BAUHAN
PUBLISHING LLC
PO BOX 117 PETERBOROUGH NEW HAMPSHIRE 03458
603-567-4430
WWW.BAUHANPUBLISHING.COM

MANUFACTURED IN THE UNITED STATES

For Wendy
and my families

ACKNOWLEDGMENTS

The author gratefully acknowledges these magazines, newspapers and media for the publication and presentation of the poems in this book, sometimes in earlier versions.

Academic Questions
Addison Independent
American Scholar
Antigonish Review
Audit
Autumn House Anthology of Contemporary American Poetry
Berkshire Review
Chariton Review
Concerning Poetry
Contemporary Poetry of New England
Denver Quarterly
Georgia Review
Joyful Noise: An Anthology of American Spiritual Poetry
Louisville Review
180 More: Extraordinary Poems for Everyday
Poetry
Poetry Miscellany
Poetry Northwest
Prairie Schooner
Seneca Review
Tendril
Virginia Quarterly Review
Voices in Wartime

INTRODUCTION

Reading a Gary Margolis poem is like being taken on a walk in a landscape, sometimes rural, sometimes urban, sometimes public, sometimes intimate, and led on a gently winding path until suddenly, one cannot quite see how it happened, one is looking out upon a huge vista from a great height, and hears the ringing of bells, joyous, majestic, ceremonial.

These are poems as ceremonies, as rites of passage. They are enactments. They provide room for events to happen and to "turn into experience" (in the words of the poet's memoir *Seeing the Songs*). In fact they do more. They enact a new kind of experience. A tangible one, as a poem, as song is. As in "Tom Verner Shows Us a Trick" "it's magic to be here / in a living room." In this "room" is made possible a containment and an expression of personal and community grief in "Below the Falls," with its transcendent final lines: "throwing / out a line, an oar, / another boy can reach."

Such poems are living experiences taking place on the page. They can be re-experienced anew with every reading. Each poem, and each reading of each poem, is a re-enactment of a negotiation between head and heart, a dialectical and open-ended event with the power to transform. The bravery of the poet is in the struggle at the limits of what can be expressed / constructed / enacted with words and of inviting the reader to witness and share in that struggle.

If the heart could conduct elegant arguments, this is much what the arguments would sound like. Not so much to say something, nor to reach a conclusion, as to listen to the voice singing in the room the poet creates. This room is a space where solitude and community can engage. Simply by the act of allowing the words, the gaps between the words, the resonances, the silences. They are linked by imagination. "Imagination isn't a reality show. Yet it is." ("What It Is We Have to Write").

And these are poems to read with the heart. Metaphor has its truest value here. Carrying the reader from one realm to another. Words become like musical notes, they ring and sing from the heart.

Josephine Dickenson
Allston, England
2013

Consider Yourself

Consider yourself
the way you would the wind.
Allow sun to approach you
so the rain can follow.
This will include caring
for things inside
of things.
Let some blossoms suppose
they are playing
into your hands.
As a rule, stones will sing.
Give what you can,
what you have been given,
what you have to give.

CONTENTS

New Poems

from **Below the Falls (2010)**

NEW POEMS

To the Redwings

Go back.
It's still
too early to
be here,
to bear
the coming
snow
on the stripes
of your wings,
too early to
sing from one
end of the field
to the other
end of the world.
Look
what happened
to the face
of the wind
how it burned
before it knew
what was good
for it,
how it didn't
know what
a frozen feather
is good for.
You don't have to
believe me.

You don't have to
trust only your own
instincts.
Or the reports
of another day
coming. Like
spring. Like
those five
green shoots
too far from
my door, early
risers pointing
to the late gray
sky. As if to
say *Listen*
to the song
the wind forgot
to sing. Go back
while there's still
a wing
of time.

The End of Football

No one can remember why it happened.
No one received any notice or was told
where to redeem their tickets. Stadiums
by the sea were swept in, and fields
in the Midwest returned to fields. It was
expected citizens would know how
to cheer for themselves and read silently,
expected wives wouldn't make too
much of this, but children would. Rules,
and flags that had been thrown to enforce
the rules, were forgotten and held in
the same esteem as grass clippings.
Groundskeepers rolled Astroturf back
into the laboratory, but not anything
green by its own nature.

Speaking of nature,
people spoke more of it.
Sows were redeemed and suckled their young
in their sties, secure in their own skins.
We didn't have to think of men as lions or bears
anymore, but giants and patriots were
another story. Cities became known again
for their statues and, in one case, for its
confluence of rivers. A lot of big men were
suddenly out of work, limping and searching
for new knees. Living with us now, we needed
them to help us remember why we left our
families, why we never prayed on Sunday.

At Matanzas Inlet,
Florida, After Driving
to Midway Airport

Even, especially and just
here, the breeze amidst
the sea roses, the roses rising
from the sand, the sand

thrown in from the sea—
you're still walking from car
to car with a rag in one hand
and roses in the other,

a sign swaying around
your neck:
VET OUT OF WORK
WILL WORK FOR FOOD

WILL WATER ROSES.
Here where I have to see
you camped on your island
street, under your underpass.

Some bruises bloom roses
and not enough to eat.
Some of us are streetwise,
lake- and seaside.

With nothing between us,
save that spit of land
here the natives call the Reach.
Where the wind isn't really a bench

and not enough to eat.
Where I have to remember
Matanzas means slaughter
and blood in the sand.

After School Working, Boston, 1963

Frost was bleeding upstairs
   in a private room. Too late

became his coming soon.
   No patient can believe

he's doomed. After school,
   I worked there, in Peter Bent

Brigham's emergency room.
   A teenager. An orderly.

A disordered orderly.
   A teenager really. Without

a word for doom.
   Word came down, even

to me, low boy, our poet
   was almost done. With no

words left, written on his
   tongue. With no one else

to wheel him out or in
   to his cold box, downstairs

below my sitting chair.
   Where I sat waiting to be

called, to push a gurney
   where it had to go.

Fishing a Pair of Sunglasses off the Net Behind Home Plate on Patriots' Day

Sometimes the title is the whole
poem. Sometimes a pair of shades
is a foul ball caught in the net and not

rolling into the cupped hands
of a fisherman, here, this season's aging
batboy. Accompanied by my section's

behind-the-plate rising and falling
song. Sometimes the game is just
an accompaniment, bait to reel us

inside the park, this green sea,
to ride the customary seventh
inning wave. To sing a singer's

ode to someone's Caroline.
Especially today when the man
standing behind me, behind my last

row, nursing his Narragansett,
looks more like Paul Revere
than himself, dressed in his

colonials. Revere—here say
Reveah—who never spilled
a beer on a fan sitting below him.

Who squinted across Boston
to the harbor, before there was
anything invented to shade his eyes.

Before he rode his cobbled
ride. Before we made a country
inside Fenway this April Monday.

Serving My Country
in Cornwall, Vermont

Hodges' blossoming apple blossoms
Littlefield's tenting horse chestnut
Dunning's random daffodils, Judy's
that is
Heineckens' pond, their hand-planted
holiday trees hand-painted Nutcracker
sign
Sparks's federal fields Kim baled before
he was gone
Sarah's stalls, Ben's baking repairing
garage
They are a pair
of Woods across town
from Patrick's pristine Stine
trails
Denny's father was born in this blue
house before I was born blue
There was never a field a Rheaume didn't
mow here. Lawrence paused
his tractor to talk to me His name
was cut, began in Reims, Champagne
Where Kelly lived an owner ago
on that ridge a cave is opening
an Abenaki stayed home in
A name is more than an untold list
There's a story there which is how
I'm here, the first Margolis
to live with a Lynch
on this Anglican acre, glebe

land still deeded to the
queen, one parcel churched
in each county we live
to cut ourselves from any
indentured word
the we of our neighborhood
Maybe Dwight will tell you
who was lost the day after
he left, the paddies
he bridged
Maybe Jud Severy will
come back from his blossoming
ground

Leading Me through
the Common

Christ, my swan, my leading
man, come in, begin again.
I'm all in. Inside is in. Step
into my feather-wooden
boat. Float by pedaling
harder, faster. The pond is
ours to skim. Our war was
won here. Common is
commonly good. A child
is God sitting inside
between my painted wings.
No one who comes here
doesn't return to shore,
wing-wrapped, more less
than sure, lighter than
the crossing air, night-
docking, city-trumpeting.

Last Night
at Meadowbrook
Pavilion

The last time I inhaled I wasn't
sitting here in the Live Free
or Die state. Wasn't sitting next

to my old bride listening to these
Woodstock rockers and breathing in
a graying, silver air. Grass is

sweeter on the other side
of the grass I can't remember anyone
saying. Isn't memory a sweet

forgettable pleasure? And remembering
where I put the keys to the car.
Or was it her heart? Forgive me

if I'm looking more at the screen
next to the stage, as if I'm in my own
high-definition living room. And not

at their actual trio on stage.
Why did Young leave them alone?
Already I'm imagining their encore,

thinking of the ride home and how wobbly
I've come to be standing up, leaning
on my wife, Wendy, and that song

this crowd will call them out to sing
about Judy and not her stone-cold
blue eyes. Her eyes I can still

see, a smoky blue—I'm hazarding
a guess—inside this pine-scented,
New Hampshire haze.

Parading the Cup

Even Paul Revere can't stay
dead and rises to the occasion
on Tremont Street, this Eighteenth

of June in the Year of Our Lord
Two Thousand and Eleven.
Who knew we would need

his engraving.
There's still room, a place
on this rising cup,

held above our team's heads,
for their names and a puck's
winning date.

The dead know who's coming
down Tremont Street
and not won by the sea.

The only sea here is us,
and all of the city, revered.
Two, if by land, is a must.

So my wife and I and our son
are today's Minutemen,
watching Lord Stanley's cup

silver the air, for less than
the minute it takes to
disappear for another year.

Before it comes back
to where we are under
the scored paper, falling

like stars, under our team's
banner, Boston's black
and gold flag.

Walking with the Wild Turkeys

How would they know
they shouldn't be standing

in the middle of the road,
September 1, 2011, the first

day of school again?
Eating stones, pebbles really,

grinding the corn they
scavenged grazing across

Sparks's field. To gain more
weight than November knows

what's good for them. To
leave a few feathers for

the children to band into
headdresses, to begin to

realize they, too, are related
to First Dawn people, here

the Abenaki and Mohawk,
related to all the big questions

of our day.
How would they know I'm just

out walking, my boots scraping
the stones, which I don't mean

for them to feel is a sound they have
to run away from this fast?

As if a new neighbor's child
is assigned one of their seats

in our country school. As if
they, too, could decide, no

matter how long it takes,
to walk with me to Washington,

D.C. Where my neighbors are
standing by the White House fence

putting up their best squawk,
a word I hope isn't taken the wrong

way. Putting their bodies in harm's
way. So when our president looks

out his tall window, he'll see enough
to decide to stop any company from

laying their pipes across our nation's
fields, he'll know there's another way

to fuel our needs. He'll write the order
not to arrest any wild turkey walking

slowly, eating what he finds left out
for him. So he can clear his throat.

Sing to the children, singing
their gobbling song.

Writing a Prescription

for Deborah Digges (1950-2009)

Oh, there was one more half-
cure left to work, a dose
untried, something one of us

could still think of, suggest.
Something natural, an herb
growing even in a ditch.

And not those stadium steps
and their thinner air,
the empty parking lot.

Oh, for the life grief gives.
A prescription for grieving
and side effects we can live

with, like living. Those flowering
weeds in the ditch the dust
picks first and tests for us.

Something to eat, boil to drink.
Almost beautiful to look at
and pick, take inside. To put

into a vase, for the time it should
take for their budding leaves to flower
into a curable death.

Faneuil Hall Marketplace

The Chinese dishwasher sitting on the bench
   appears to be on break, leaning his head on his
arms, trying to make a pillow of his uncomfortable

   elbow. Although I only think, say, he's Chinese,
because he's sitting next to a sign that includes
   a row of characters I cannot read. Does it make

a difference where I think he's from? Any country
   of his may not have had room for him. I'm afraid
if I sit down, I'll wake him, and he probably

   only has a few more minutes to make a good night's
sleep out of his nap. I'm guessing I wouldn't have
   anything to say to him the two of us could understand,

I'm that uncomfortable. But who's to say, without
   saying anything, we both would know what the other
meant. That something was said here once to wake up

a nation about tea and taxes, about speaking up
no matter what, about two- and three-cornered hats,
   John Hancock's speech and Li Po's silent art.

Not Taxing the Marathon

Imagine fifteen thousand runners
in front of you in the revolutionary
town of Hopkinton, Massachusetts,
on Patriots' Day, April 19th.

And the only wall between you
and Boston Harbor is more than
a marathon and a hill full of heart-
break away. Not one hill but three,

rising from tree-lined Newton
to the half-sober students of
B.C. at Chestnut Hill,
lining the race's route

with cans and jeers, cheering
you might break down, hit
the wall, those bricks
in the heart where your will

is muscle-weary. They're full
of last night's sobering
history and wobble here
so they don't have to open

a book for a while. You might
be sicker than you thought
trying to run while looking out
to the sea of bodies making a tide

of rolling waves, oscillating,
you could say, if you could say
anything. If you weren't trying
to catch your breath, let alone those

Patriots, John Kelley and Bill
Rodgers, who finished hours
ahead of you, who are wearing,
not sitting on, their laurels

and drinking beer, not tea.
Who have enough heart to wait
for you and eventually all
the revolving Kenyans to come,

starting with Ibrahim Hussein and
Catherine Ndereba.
If the light wasn't losing itself
in the winning sea

and the police weren't waving
those students, those Eagles, back
into their dormitories, weren't letting
cars return to their roped-off streets.

At the Derry Frost Farm

Someone keyed their name
into one of the tilting field
stones near today's dried-up
Hyla Brook. Someone who

wasn't afraid to ruin the wall,
to leave a few letters for the snow
to erase. How does a stone become
a stone again, he isn't here to say.

A key scratching a falling, once-
placed rock is all is said and done.
We, too, want to think no one was here,
before we came, before we turned

off the major road and drove to
the other side of Derry. Alan Shepard's
side, we guessed, our first thrown man
into space. He might have said

pitched like a moon-bruised batted
baseball, erasing a fence.
(Here, I have to say, if we were
standing in Fenway's Park,

he could have thought
There's a city that loves its wall,
loves to throw stones
over a monster fence.)

Our Shepard astronaut found
his way down to earth through a hole
in the clouds and didn't burn.
Isn't that what a stone is for?

To scratch something on another
stone, for time to tell. So when one
of us returns, he'll know where
he is, she'll know where she was.

Face Value

We print more on a press
in the basement.
My wife is my president.

The mint made a precedent
of printing a man's face
on a roll of paper.

My wife is my papyrus.
Her love is my stylus.
We save face in our

basement. We vote
to devote more time
to face time, to exchange

our coins, our change,
for bills.
To roll with it.

Gays adorn our continental
army. Three of a kind
is a good hand. Once

we had a full house
and didn't charge for it,
one pharaoh at a time.

Let's face it.
Let's bank on it.
Let's lift our president

from her basket.
Let's play
Hail to the Chief

on our reed
instrument.
No one says

we can't vote her in
hands-down.
No one believes our

country couldn't break
a bill with her
face on it.

We don't need a bill
for that. Only
a personal

engraver and a press.
Revere etched
his wife in the basement,

engraving her.
The Bay is our bowl.
We're our own colony,

a family currency.
My neighbor, tour
the mint in my cellar.

Come over for supper.
Don't think you'll have to
pay for it. Don't mind

asking if that's mint
in the tea and a new
sea of bills floating

up from my basement.
My love and I are flooding
the market.

Isn't love what we can't
make of it, its own
reverence?

My love isn't sitting
for her portrait.
Her eagle is my wren.

Isn't love an anthem
meant to be heart-
wrenching, unmistakable,

unprecedented?
An army of lips
fêted.

Cy's Podium

This year, it's not here.
    It's loaned, down
the road, to Whiting,
    our near enough next
town. When we need it
    most. When we need
Cy, our March town
    moderator, to lean on us
to speak up, civilly, to cast
    our voice-raised votes.
She's standing there
    alone, tall enough to see
out to us, when we raise
    our hands. So she can call
on one of us to stand,
    Norman Rockwellish.
Here in our children's
    Cornwall gym. Next
to a field the cows,
    Holsteins, still wander in.
To see who's raising her
    hand, speaking up.
Without a podium to stand
    behind. Who's saying all
he can, in front of neighbors
    he agrees to live next door to,
even when there are good things
    they disagree on. Except
the right of our firemen,
    say firefighters, our next-door

men and women, to now
    walk in, between votes, carrying
Cy's podium, Whiting-returned.
    Say what we're here for.
Say what we've, one vote
    at a time, town- and city-bred,
earned.

To the Nun I Sat Next to in Summer School Class after Failing Biology Lab

You're beautiful in your habit,
pure black and white. Who wouldn't
want to make a habit of you, by

imagining what you're like.
The maple pours gold inside
if you stay up all night boiling

down its sap. And praying
you'll let me say what I feel,
keeps me up at night. Gold is all

that's left of burning leaves.
That cross on your belt is crossing me.
I'd be one bead on your string

of prayers, if you'd tell me to believe
the blood of our frog is really Christ's.
That together we'll look inside

at what we're meant to see—
a body and a ghost—the answer
we'll have to know to sex,

forgive me, the dead,
if we're meaning to pass
this station's course.

Retirement Isn't the Same
as Vacating the Vatican

My pope is going to live
    with the nuns. In the Vatican's
nunnery. Together they'll
    have a lot of fun praying

the ceiling won't come down.
    He's tired enough to retire.
My granddaughter says
    our pope is all pooped out.

She likes the way a prayer
    fools around on her tongue.
And asks me if a grandfather
    can be a nun, if I'm too tired

to play. If, in retirement,
    I'll learn to paint
lying on my back, dripping
    paint on my face.

Once, I asked a beautiful nun-
    to-be if she believed in the Beatles.
We were sitting in lab
    sharing a frog. She looked at me

as if I were Michelangelo.
    As if I would make a habit
of asking her this.
    This is what I believed

when I was young enough
    to tell the truth. When I prayed
on my knees. I tell my granddaughter
    when you're old you can't stand up.

You have to sit in a chair to look up
    to the sky. To see God-in-the Clouds
reaching out. To believe the coin
    in your hand is the sun.

Confession

I have more books than anyone could
read in a library of lifetimes.
Many are still in their fresh
jackets, their pages stitched
together by an invisible hand.
Many are written in a language,
I lie to myself, I'll take the time
to learn. Farsi and Modern
Hebrew are two coming to mind.
Most days I sit in a room where they are,
which is everywhere, and browse
their titles, worrying what they think of
a would-be reader. Thinking, if I pulled
a century of all-nighters, I could relieve
the tension between us, I could go
freely into my book-bagged afterlife
I have to admit is a bookstore,
a church basement, as bizarre as that might
sound. Where my neighbors have been
bringing their unread books, and marking
them down, so far down, for next summer's
bazaar, it's as if they're giving them away.
As if they are carrying a bagful
of remorse for trucking them from the happiness
of their shelves, away from their printed
shelf life.

Suspension
for Lawrence Raab

Probably it's next to impossible
to ask your dream to remember
the punch line, to restore the entire

joke just from its first few lines.
*A man walked into a donkey
store*... isn't enough some nights

to hold your head on the pillow,
not to wake your wife to see
what she has to say, to build

the bridge that donkey is
reluctant to cross. A dream
is born to balk when it can.

And there's only so much
you can ask of yourself,
of a sleep-dreaming joke,

so much you can expect to know,
take from that beast
for whom *burden* isn't a word

he would think of himself.
A woman walked into a dream
might be another possibility

if you aren't into donkeys,
if you don't believe everything
we see and hear, we feel, has its way

of crossing the rope bridge
between day and night, between
the first line and the last.

It's all about timing, my wife
says in her sleep, speaks
into her pillow, when I nudge her,

when she mumbles something
about *suspending…flickering
flies…a man walking…*

Festival on the Green

Maybe we'll bump into
each other again.
Chance is choice.

Maybe the past will march
across the green.
A soldier stands in his

statue.
Maybe we can sleep out
there. If a festival makes

more of us
than the music
means to.

The hill is a folding chair.
Maybe we'll see a band
in the bandstand.

And not a ring
of wild, dancing
children.

Not a plaque
with names and dates,
what didn't happen

here. Maybe the colonel
will step off his stone
pedestal before the last

set. Before the volunteers
walk among us, offering
their baskets.

Over the Fence

for Paul Witteman (1943-2013)

Two seats saved from Tiger
   Stadium. Attached. Detroit blue.
Once nailed to his deck in Hart's

Neck. His New Jersey, New York,
   Maine. So when we're there, one
of us could sit with him to see

the tide cover the mud
   infield again, meaning the sea
filling in the story of what

we have to guess is out there,
   over the fence, Paul, our reporter,
might have said. Our Witteman.

Would have wanted us to feel
   the slatted seat, the metal armrest,
as if we were sitting in a box

seat on a Sunday afternoon.
   With nothing between us, save
saying a few things we could

take home like ticket stubs,
   like a score we came to forget.
That didn't seem anything

like the countless waves,
   coming in, going back.
Leaving that boat sitting

on the flat, like a ball
   someone could catch
in the parking lot

on the other side
   of the fence.
Someone like Paul,

who wanted us to know
   what it's like to sit
in Tiger Stadium.

A Kind of Country

Into this neutral air
Where blind skyscrapers use
their full height to proclaim...
September 1, 1939, W.H. Auden

Oh bricklayers, window glazers,
steel makers. Wire splicers, pipe
fitters.

Oh high-rise air walkers,
safety inspectors, basement dwellers,
office decorators.

Oh building builders, ground
and sky bound, saw grinding,
midnight oil burning, outside,
inside September workers.

All ash-sweeping hall sweepers,
elevator-stranded spider strands,
typing typists, receptionists
receiving.

All hands on our flag-decorated deck.
Bell, not hand-wringing.
Gardeners in the courtyard planting
willow-sweeping sidewalk sweepers.

Oh now forever moment's weeping
red remembering. Not just flag-
waving memory. Bricks and glass,
plastic, steel and paper shredding.
Street-running, avenue-filling.
A kind of country love-making,
grave-digging miracle in
the making.

World of Good

In the beginning I hated
the Yankees God gave us.
Until I came to see Derek Jeter,
their shortstop, go deep

into the hole, lift off
his infield, twirl and, in one
impossible motion, throw
my beloved out. Without

appearing to ask anything
in return. Not that my hate
turned to love. Or that I would
tell anyone at the time,

I sometimes saw myself in
pinstripes, too, stripped of my
Boston birthright to boo
anyone who played in a borough,

who walked, no, strolled, the way
millionaires do, up to the plate.
And not that I'm afraid to say
from the beginning, I despised

their star Rodriguez. Not that I really
wished he would die or have something
befall him I wouldn't be able to take
back into my heart, forgive myself for.

Not that kind of hateful hate.
When I cursed his bat, shouting
a phrase a fan understands is not
to be taken personally, mean

more than it means.
Helping him to hit nothing
but air, turning these words
into a world of good.

It's you they come to
for my colleagues in the college health service

in the middle of the night,
coughing and staggering,
fearing they are about

to fail. Wanting to say
something, sometimes,
their bodies are saying

for them. Isn't that
what you're here for, too?
To listen to the wheezing

songs inside their chests,
to sing something a mother,
a father might sing,

if only they were here,
If only they knew
what you're bound to keep

to yourselves most
of the time. I mean,
there are times you have

to tell someone else, if they
are to save their own lives.

And I am one of you.
Who thinks of these students,

our patients, not *as if*
they live upstairs in a room

in my house, but because,
at night, after a shift, I'm still
thinking of them, I still hear

what they said, I had to
document. In case someone
would be listening later,

or they, too, might want to read
what I heard in their own
words. Often it's late

when they come in, not too
late. And you tell me,
on this eve of my closing

my door, how you are still
amazed, some mornings,
when the sun is rising

over the breath of our
Green Mountains,
when another student is

coming or going,
how well you feel, doing
what you do, when
you know what you have
done. When no one is
around to see.

Inviting the Dalai Lama
to Cornwall, Vermont

Why wouldn't you want to walk down
  Sperry Road with your entourage?

See the rolled bales, a piece of their
  plastic wrap strewn like a scarf

in the field, in your tongue a *khata,*
  a silk-white blessing. Smell

the unpicked, fallen apples
  the wind drops into our fall

syrup, a kind of honey the yellow
  jackets forget to sting.

Why wouldn't you want to
  listen to the cows lowing

in their pasture, find Belle—
  83 pierced through her ear—

standing near her barbed fence,
  gazing, not gawking

at your maroon robe, at
  the petals thrown on the path

before you like stones
    Stu Johnson, our commissioner

of roads, grades into our road?
    Why wouldn't you want to

feel at home here, the Adirondacks
    our Himalayas, the Green Mountains

a parade of foothills really, for
    a few of the town's llamas to graze,

a shadow to coax the moon over?
    Here where my neighbors and I will

learn to bring one palm to the other,
    before you arrive. Will remember

why you are here and not home
    in the snow-filled bowl of the world,

sitting in Tibet, weaving a chant,
    singing the name of your enemy.

My Annual Appeal
to the Louvre

I'm appealing to you
personally, my gift,
my director, to sell one
of your priceless paintings
in your personal collection
and donate everything you
receive to the John Graham
Shelter here in Addison
County, Vermont.
Where even at the end
of the year when funds
are low our homeless
residents are sitting
like models—no disciples—
around a table full
of donated vegetables
and other goods.
Where what they are
given is not a given.
Although if you've ever
responded to an annual
appeal outside your
vintage window, you
know how your heart
is left happily unguarded
at the end of the year.
Of course, I wouldn't expect

you not to worry about setting
an impossible precedent,
year after year, and, I confess,
I'm writing the director
of the Gardner Museum
in Boston, too, expecting her
to break Isabella's will
to allow the sale of her priceless
Rape of Europa, Titian's
god-filled bull. So a city
of street people can eat.
So a boulevard can forget,
mon Dieu, it's a bed.
So there's a window
to see to our angels
of painted hills.

My President's Nearby

Look at the helicopters chopping
the sky. He's running more
than our sap is. His men are
running alongside.
He's somewhere waving

inside, prompting me to
wave back, to believe
he's inside. My president
won't be back, so I'd better
line the street with my sign.

Maybe I'm the vote he needs.
Maybe he likes real syrup
on the side. Maybe I'll win
the lottery and pay to go in
to hear what he has to say.

There's an old saying
The last time a president
was here, Ethan Allen walked
across the Lake.
I don't doubt Doubt is my

democracy. Even from here
at the front of the gym,
he's prompted to wave,
to see my vote rising
to Burlington's occasion.

Naming the Perpetrator

Stone by stone,
you're not allowed

in. You're not my
fence, my allowance

my broken
words. Here's

my sword for you
to fall on, all

of you. It's my
honor to

stone you word
by word.

Your name is
named.

I memorize
my memories.

My body is
a thrown

stone.
I can take you

out. Outside
is in. Now you

know what
you're in

for. I live
inside a falling

wall, stone by
stone. I am my

David, not
your army.

Forgetting is
building a hand-

made wall
a name lives

inside.
Remembering

is my name's
shadow all

alone. My heart
is posted.

Shells walk
my land

expended.
My love is orange-

invested, red-leafed,
far-branching.

Raking Buddha's Leaves

And you came to the shade
of the Bodhi tree, here a maple.

To sit in the shade. To feel
the breath of your breathing.

To see your thoughts settle,
leaf by leaf. As if they had

nothing to say. As if they
weren't yours, but

the world's. What I'm
thinking, this afternoon,

raking a wind's worth
of maple leaves into

a pile for burning. What
could be called my mind.

If it weren't for the birds,
here a mouthful of cedar

waxwings, calling,
Master, our mouths are

empty.
Master, what are you

thinking?
We can't eat the leaves

of your thoughts.
We can't sit still

until we are full.
And isn't that what

the world's saying,
I think I hear the blue jay

shrieking, I think I see
in the leaves burning,

feeding the fire,
becoming what they were?

Vermont Magnetic Field

Praise to the weird way
the geese spiral back,
not lost exactly or spinning

in the wind
yet taken by a new
sunny direction.

Praise to the unsettling
leaves left to their own
discretion to swirl around

our heads. *Paper planets*
you could say, if you didn't
mind being accused of thinking

like a dog walking around in
circles, his left eye ticking
like a faucet, clearly disoriented,

clearly looking for a pond
to walk on. Praise to the Roman
way all roads lead to Rome,

today the home of the Exploding
Sun, a good name for a team
in the Coliseum if it weren't

for the bones they would have
to run around, blood bleaching
its stones. If it weren't true

today we receive praise
from the flaring sun—Solar
Storm—another good name

a team hasn't taken, sworn
to lay down their lives for.
However weird it is, we look

to the heavens for our particular
future, for that spinning ball
honking toward us.

Springtime in Boston

All winter we look forward
to lounging on the couch
after dinner, no way, really,

to trumpet the beginning
of a poem. Yet the best way
I have of saying how much

we adore each other in summer,
when the evenings stretch
a few extra innings,

what we hope for tonight,
as we lie here, not knowing
what to do with our team

which hasn't found a way
to win, as May turns to June.
As you turn to me

with a look I've come
to know. *Forlorn* isn't
exactly the word,

though it's close enough
to what I'm feeling, too.
Although you wouldn't know it,

by the way I cheer us to
believe our next run is only
one hit away. If you promise

not to get up and say you have
better things to do than lie
here until October next to me.

That the garden needs weeding,
in the dark. And even our love
can take only so much losing.

Tom Verner Shows Us
a Trick

Even sitting this close
to his impromptu
improbable stage, to see

inside his sleeve, behind
his back, something tells you
to believe, not second-guess

that's fire flaming from his
tricky book. That arm-
length pin is really piercing

his trick balloon. All we're in
is in his living room, believing
what he says,

when his wand becomes
a flowering book and then
a pen again in a writing room.

Pinned or penned,
it's magic to be here
in a living room. Leaves

soaking through the window
sill. Wood stacked and green.
Too green to burn.

Finishing the Term

That student lost his legs below his knees,
had them taken from him. And today
he's sitting in his moving chair in the lobby

of the library. With the usual traffic
of borrowers, coming and going.
Surrounded by the decision whether

to find a quiet chair, a carrel, and get
down to business. Or wheel himself
for a few minutes among the open

stacks, stopping to browse a book
he has no use for this semester.
Which can only get him into some

save-the-work-for-later trouble.
Isn't that why we leave home, go to
school, even study abroad?

Even when we don't know
what we will gain, what we will lose.
Like opening that book he takes

from the shelf, puts on his lap.
Trying to decide, you can see
I'm imagining, whether he should

begin reading now or later.
What would do him more good, I can't
say in the long run, but now

when he's expected to write
his essay, to study what he can only
guess will be asked of him.

What It Is We Have
to Write
for the Bread Loaf Young Writers' Conference

Someone's standing before you,
holding a key to his heart,
who sat where you're sitting,

listening to a writer speak
about writing.
Some keys are clues to the dark

and doors to the heart.
Let's start, before it gets dark.
Let's not forget this isn't

an assignment. Writing makes you
an upstart, but not here.
I've already started to say

Don't be afraid to start again,
to erase what you thought
you wrote.

My teacher taught me to think
with chalk in my hand.
Some words rise in its dust.

Don't be surprised you feel
a lump in your throat
when you hear what you've felt

in someone else's lines.
Be surprised as much as you can,
when you're standing in line

in the Inn, thinking of what you heard,
what you can write.
I hope it's not surprising to think

of yourself as a writer.
And that doe I suddenly see
in the back field while I'm writing

disappears faster than a feeling.
Isn't that what the field of a page
is for? More often than not

a page is also a door into
the dark. A pen is a key.
Here's where I'm supposed

to say, *Don't keep your random*
thoughts, your dreams to yourself.
They need your page.

They need to live outside
your heart. Once I dreamt
I'd be standing here. I can't

keep that to myself.
Frost stood outside the doors.
Or I thought he did.

He used to say, *I'm going
to say a poem to you.*
And did. You're here

to say the words you brought
to someone you've never met
before. *Be amazed they understand,*

they take you to heart. Here
we can say what we think,
even if no one has ever said it.

Even if that image of a doe
isn't the way you'd express
a disappearing feeling.

In fact, I hope it's not.
In fact, I hope there isn't
a fact you wouldn't imagine

differently, you wouldn't turn
into your own beautiful
reality. Imagination isn't

a reality show. Yet it is.
Hope dances in your notebooks.
And who doesn't want to lose

some weight, without losing?
Who doesn't want to be the last
survivor, taking notes in a diamond

notebook? *Look around you,*
if you want to see a theater-full
of survival stories, a few hundred

islands. *Guess what the writer*
sitting next to you is beginning
to imagine she wants to write next.

Did I call you a writer? *Give me*
one good reason why not.
Give me all you've got in writing.

And, forgive me, I hope I haven't
forgotten to speak, for a moment,
like a jock, like a poet taking off

his cleats in a locker room.
In my school, on my team,
I couldn't tell anyone

I held a notebook next to my heart.
I couldn't say really what hurt,
my reality. I hope I'm not hiding

in the woods behind a doe.
And yet isn't the woods
where we go, sometimes,

when we want to be alone
with a clean page? Or our room.
A little-known gallery

in the city museum.
A coffee shop. A movie
theater. Anywhere you can be

alone with your loneliness.
James Wright, one of my teachers,
wrote, seeing two Indian ponies across

the road, *There is no loneliness
like theirs*. Every day I think of
what he said. I think I can love

my loneliness, when I'm sitting
next to someone in the dark, looking
at a painting that feels like it takes up

the whole room. Or when I become
aware that doe is looking at me
from her woods. Wouldn't I see

Frost in the window, if I came back
in a different season? I'm not saying
you should like what Frost wrote,

or anything, by anyone. Only that
you take a moment, say over these
few days we have together, to see

what you thought to write in lines,
poetry and prose, to see what you
made up, to make of your lives.

See what you can take home to
your own woods, even when
there are no woods nearby.

I'm not trying to take you
by surprise totally when I say
now (by now you know

I'm writing this,) when I put
the Lakota prayer in my mouth
and pray, *Mitakuye Oyasin,*

We are all related.
Here, at Bread Loaf, in the woods
of our words. In things we keep

to ourselves and may write later.
Much, much later,
when we least expect to need

that doe standing at her door.
When there's blood in our hearts
and leaves to lie down on.

When we look around and can't
find a pen, a clean piece of paper,
and fear rises like dust.

When we remember who we were
sitting next to this first conference
night, and what it is we have to write.

Packing for Eternity

There's nothing you'll need to save
for the afterlife you won't be able
to ask for once you are there.

It's not like going to overnight camp
with a list of items to help you survive
in the woods, a duffel bag of

socks and shorts, two dress
T-shirts. Even the angels,
it was written, were sent away

in July for a few weeks
by a lake, a few nights to sleep
under the stars without any feeling

of responsibility to think of them
as God. Even the angels,
you were told, felt homesick

for a few hours their first night
away. And cried into their
pillows, so no one could hear them

finding a way to be brave.
No one knows if it will be any
different than what you know

now. And didn't summer used to
feel like an eternity? And sleeping
under the stars a place you didn't

want to go home from?
Sometimes we make too much
of what we don't know and turn it

into a mystery. Sometimes we spend
our whole lives thinking about
what's to come, making a list

of things in a million years we
wouldn't need. Like that compass
and skeleton key, that extra crown.

Raking the Winter
Leaves

There should be snow by now,
ice packing the eaves, the gutters,
and not this lawn, still green, leaves

strewn, branches where drifts are used
to being. The wind is arguing again
in Washington what's causing this.

While here, in Vermont, we're used to
saying the fields are open, we're having
an open winter, like an open house,

when any weather is welcome to come
over. And we're not electing anyone
to credit, to blame our volunteering

sun. It takes a long time for the new
sun to shine native. Science is one
of our natures. Which doesn't mean

we don't have to pay attention to
what's causing us to say it's because
of you the earth is too green here,

the snow is forgotten. Because of
you I won't have you over to rake my
winter leaves, the wind can sweep in.

from *The Day We Still Stand Here* (1982)

August

These are the days we go away,
before September sharpens its pencil,
opens its lined and yellow pages.
We arrange to be on another coast,
its tides dragging the hours
back and forth over the bottom,
to be under the cast of a new
locality, charmed by its accent
and acceptance. We are never here
long enough to knot these habits,
and our children, too, suspend
themselves for now, in the rented
dream they are related as cousins.
Even when fog threatens to stay
and does, it covers everything,
and the wires of disappointment
become too wet to pass current.
Away from responsibility, the times
held for making love are held,
and signs that say, now, there's
time, find us looking for them.
Yet even before we leave, at night,
the lawn, the stacked mail begin
to tug on the ropes we forgot
to untie. The road already starts
our car without us and, before we know it,
we have never gone away again.

Geese Overhead

If you wait to hear them, their voices
will not come down.

If you remember to listen, they draft
behind clouds, a blinding angle to the sun.

As you pull squash, warty and gone by,
cornstalks point to their going.

Slowly changing the flight of their arrow,
each flaps into a small bow,

and wind, pulling them further,
rattles the dry vines, pointing you

in their direction. Now one flies
to the lead, two drop to the middle

where the same strength is needed,
an old drake drifts to the end. There emptiness

is a sea. It loves to lose
the weak, the furthest out, the forgetful.

Passions of the Flowering Apple

In Cornwall, we have the longest
growing season in Vermont.
Wind carries the lake across the fields,
ripens our herbs. So we hurry the wind.
Now, in September, bees return
empty, their wings free of flower
dust. They have farmed the goldenrod
and store their honey,
feed their brood.

Have you ever seen the berries
of the ash so red,
the branches of the apple
so full and low to the ground?

Across the hill, Jamaicans,
singing their light songs,
pick through the orchards.
I hear the one
wearing a new watch
rolls apples down his arms
into his basket,

each a note in the air.
I wish I had his voice.

But I have you
and the box elders out back
you say, each fall, are a pair,

one full of seeds, the other without.

We were like them,
and when wind blew, nothing
fell out of us onto the ground.

Today, I see fruit the apple
has given you to carry, to flower
in the longest growing season in Vermont.

When wind comes in March,
when sap runs and calls the crocus up,
gather a basket.

This is the year a bud will bear.
This is the day we still stand here.

I Am Ordered to Go
and Say So Long

I

We marry.

The Army, an old flame,
sends love.

Father decorates mother.
Mother moves up a grade.

Major mother.

I wire myself
regards and dance,
welcoming well-wishers,
pleasing my uncles who come
from far away.

Occasionally
the band stops
playing our song

and I sing

as if I believe
in anything.

2

I leave because war says
Trust me. At night
on patrol,
I am careless.
My light is seen miles
from here.
Dropping my compass,
I give myself away.

Your letters are a string
of broken ponies
coming up lame.
Some of them I open
and give to orphans.
Some of them I read.
Each says, *Bastard, get home.*

War never says one thing
and means another.
It is not my wife,
taking too much
of my bed, telling me
to turn off the light.
It comes once and says
The rest is up to you.

During the War

After dinner, we walked beside the city's river,
arm in arm, talking where the current took us.
The avenues were empty, the plazas, their great buildings
and fountains quiet, except for an occasional light

high in one of the office windows
where an accountant leaned over his figures.
We stopped on your street, and back in your room
the history of men and women asked to be remembered.

If only the river was longer and wound
through the shadows of town on toward dawn.
If only it ended in the outskirts,
in the soft corner of a field,

we would have been able to lie down
and continue the comforting with our hands, our talk,
like others whose gentle steps took them there.
What happened was all right, only faster.

But when we were done, we could not return.
There was no river to follow, just trampled sheets
and the footprints of those before us,
who gave up their arms and abandoned their boots.

Stateside

When your chopper lands here
you are halfway home.

I see the fire
on your face is out.

No smoke rises
from your fingers.

If you look up
through bandages

into the warm night
haze, I am another

gauze, another day,
stamping the smoldering grasses

which now in Texas
are not the slender shoots

of rice bending wind,
not the tiger lilies of Long Binh.

I Appraise the Probability
of Improving

I call the day nurse
Night
sometimes Good Night.
I see her first
a fitted sheet
and she is last
to leave
straightening each bit
asking *Is there anything*
you need?
She checks my chart
the bend in the bed
and puffs the pillows.
She is pleased
with my progress.
Between day and night
the relief shift
feeds me by hand.
The girls rotate
so I never know
who will walk in
whose voice will come
over the intercom.
The same man buffs
the floors.
I hear him humming
with his machine.

The night nurse brings
tape and pills.
She never changes
except on weekends
when they find
no one regular
to replace her.
She says *Open*
and I do.
I would never
call her
Good Day.

Her Room
after Andrew Wyeth

It is difficult to say exactly
why the door is open.
To let the sea breeze in?
But why, then, are the two
front windows closed?
Perhaps someone has left
in a hurry and for good?
A conch rests on a pine
chest, the only furniture
in sight. Not rests, really,
but is placed, so half is shadow,
half emanates its own light.
The curtains, pulled back
to their middles, are pink,
pale enough to see through.
Sunlight slants onto
the open door,
carrying a yellow hue.
This afternoon,
the sea calms into a cove,
and a neck of pines,
out there as a coast,
confirms this. Under the window
nearest the door, a row
of shells, small to large,
suggests children.

What more can we know
or say from what has been
given us to see?
Even the pine, with just
the tips of its branches
visible, says something of
the absences with which we are left.
Everything is as important
as anything else—the door,
the windows, the chest,
the shells and the sea,
even the light, its long
casting from the west.
Is this the room
where she sleeps,
or the place she rocks time,
looking out, the room
anyone who knows her
would say is hers?

The Carver

At Six Nations, the Grand River thins
to a string of blue beads.
After a brief rain flowering lupine,
Jacob Sky brings his son into the woods
to look for a young larch
the width of his grandfather's face.
He finds one opening leaves and begins
singing a family song, how a woman
loses teeth and a daughter
chews meat for her. The boy laughs,
turns toward his father carving
the split eyes, hooked nose, out from the trunk.
They drop the tree and leave it to dry.
Water empties back into the body
of the sky. In those hours, lips part,
eyes open for a finch to fly through,
barely brushing his wings.
By night, the mouth moves.
Whistling the windy melody of the river,
they return the next day
and carry it on a branch between them.
When they reach home, the youngest girl
puts up her dolls, disappears
behind the house. Twelve horsetails
hang in the late sun. She chooses one
and tacks the hair to fall
on either side of the crooked face.
Her mother brings a bowl of mashed berries

for the children to rub into lips
and cheeks, raising a true color.
Then they hoist it onto a pole
facing the Iroquois sun,
and it is made again, done for this season,
surely as the wind lends words for the mask to sing.

Ananda's Talk with Buddha

His cousin and favorite disciple, Ananda, is credited with
having persuaded Buddha to admit women into his order.

Cousin, the wind sleeps in a cave when you speak.
Rain falls to Vihara. Each vine blossoms
with melons familiar as prayer.
How ripe red is! Women wash inside you,
bathe their feet by your flowing heart.
They are scents of lilac and cypress,
the blue beads in water. Ask yourself,
have you not washed with their leaves and been clean,
blessed yourself, praising the river?
This question will clothe you, shell of the moon,
orchid of every name, cousin of comfort and rain.

Back

The side with no face,
no mouth or eyes.

The exact picture of someone
always leaving.

Outline of blades
under a cotton shirt.

The shelf of shoulders
bending under weight.

And tonight
when stars return

lying down on the earth
we can face them.

Town Meeting

In a recent survey, when asked
what they most feared, the majority
answered, speaking in front of others.
Death was number seven.
Today, across our state, in town meetings,
we give ourselves another chance
to decide what to make of our lives,
how to spend what we have earned
farming, teaching, selling our stores,
staying home with the children, our first work.
Far from here, within range
of our voice's vote, bombs are being built,
set, it seems lately, on the trigger
of a spider's web we have each seen
in the eave of a barn, a glass star
spun overnight, the spinning
that ties dew and beam together.
Or set on the idea that others, whose
names we could once pronounce
(they were our own) build more bombs
than we and have no reason not to let
them go, because, we think, they have
nothing to lose. Or so we are told.
They, too, used to knock down their webs
with a broom, and now, like us, are more
likely to leave them alone, let the light pass

through. Today we ask, What is the best way
to defend ourselves, to spend our taxes,
in Cornwall, in Bristol, in Buel's Gore,
not a town, but where people meet as well.
Some will argue this is not the right place
to discuss this (we are too close to home),
and not the right time (we have other business—
our roads, the school budget, whether we
want to add on to the library), or that
we have elected others to decide this for us,
who know more than we do about
what happens when a fly lands on
any one of the wires of a spider's web,
here in Vermont, where flies
cluster like burdock and move slowly as syrup;
what happens when a herd of Holsteins,
their bags full, almost cross Route 7,
as we wait, watching fly, cow, and burr,
who will be left after us to speak.

from *Falling Awake* (1986)

Knock Back

The smallest of them, the downy,
learned to cling to a suet net
as if it were bark and pick at

the beef fat until spring returned
its store of eggs and grubs.
All through history, and thus

literature, men and women have been
cursed and blessed into trees
when they tried to run away

from their lives. The birds didn't
care, except the downy woodpecker,
who, it appeared, had something more

in mind, trying to drill himself
down to the elm's clogged heart.
It's not that I could just imagine

hearing him, like a miner alive under
the hand of the mine's timbers,
but more what I knew I was in

store for. Once, out walking, I saw
the shell of an elm in front of me
and how, in one step, I would catch

up with my tree-life, cursed and
blessed into a trunk and branches
the downy woodpecker would drum on,

until either the elm hummed, or full
and still, and finally still myself,
he could hear my breath knock back.

Pearl of the Moon

For three days I cried
the dry tears of worry.
And then I wept for a week
until I was floating
on my own pond of tears.

I saw cove lilies open
and close, and the loon
open the mouth of the pond
and disappear, only to rise
later in his sister's

hollow song. Each night
the moon cast more
of its pearls,
until the whole pearl
of the moon hung

like a song from my neck.
Old saw-whet owl would
tu from the woods
when he saw the moon
singing in the water.

Tears meant nothing to him
but more water in which
to see the moon's song.
When wind dragged in
the night clouds,

he tried to fly above them
to find the singing
necklace of the moon,
and almost died in the branchless
forest of the clouds.

I cried for three days,
until the pond strung
all of my tears
for that saw-whet owl
to wear, too.

Slow Words for Shoreham
and the Apple Blossom Derby

All the runners and near-runners start
to stretch the night before, to push against
the nearest wall in their sleep, then bend over
clasping the backs of their calves like swanning
ballerinas. Here in Shoreham's apple country,
the annual spring run begins again in the May
blossom of their minds. Back inside the year
these local running friends see the year go

off across a chalked-in starting line, starting
in a church parking lot and running the falling
hills nearly five miles down to Lake Champlain
and the reversing Ticonderoga ferry. The race
organizers try to time the run to coincide
with when the millionth apple blossom breaks
open and the route is a safe paradise from
pollinating bees. History tells them the first

hill is the quiet killer, a quarter down
and three quarters up to the revolutionary
cemetery overlooking the blistered lake.
But then, as it is said at the marathon in mother
Boston, after Heartbreak Hill, it's all downhill
from there. In between the untimed meadows,
the saintly, dumbfounded Holstein cows each
year come more and more to look like Woody

Jackson's mindful paintings of them.
Down across the temporary finish line
to the only stone building nearby the water
holding its share of lead shot and blood—
which still runs over these bursting apple hills—
they run by and stop to remember who,
out of breath, shoeless and unnumbered,
lay down and finished before them.

Away from Any Uniform

During the war when I needed to cry
I would drive to the nearest airport
and watch the soldier sons and some

daughters come home or say good-bye.
In the common privacy of the terminal
they were free to weep in the company

of strangers. Before the war, it took
going to a movie in which something went
wrong between a father and his son

for me to feel my throat tighten, my eyes
well up. The only time I saw my father
cry was when his father died. Too much

had gone wrong between them for him
to want to fly back and bury that war.
I don't think the families minded me

watching or even knew their tears could
start mine flowing. In their eyes I was
another loved one waiting for his to come

back or leave. Now with us only half at war,
I've had to learn to cry away from any
uniform or family that isn't mine.

When a plane drones overhead trailing
the tearless smoke of its jet stream,
and my son looks up, who's seen enough

of war in play and on the news to know
some sons go away and die, I let him see
this tear he can take back to his wounded sky.

For the Woman at the Fast-Food
Fish Place Who Called Me Pig

In this place God leaves His morsels unguarded—
crumbs on the breadboard, an extra French fry
left on the cashier's counter, and now the colorful
and extravagant unlocked salad bar I not-so-

innocently graze, waiting for my take-out fish to cook.
Out of the corner of your eye, more than mother-like,
you notice my grazing—I think I am at home—and
turn your fork into a gavel, your raincoat into

a judge's robe. When I feel hungry or guilty, guess
which one wins? My hand floats over the carrot sticks
and bacon bits to the innocent croutons. I know
this franchise boasts nationally its charcoal-broiled

techniques, but the flames I feel are dragon flames,
spewing over me from your booth. Beyond the rhyme,
I'm conscious my snitching is uncouth, my hand so
unsanitary you wish the plastic sneeze guard would crash

like a guillotine. The last broccoli spear I take
is the straw that calls your army out, in full chain mail,
visors down, shields up. You march to the teenage
assistant manager and report my deeds by amount

and appetizing category. Handing over my fish and fries,
he looks to me for some assurance her eyes
will not find a sin of his for condemnation. Seeing
he does not choose or is too young to reprimand

my public cheating, she turns to me and, in a whisper
louder than one God found in His Big Way to turn
Adam out, she brands me Pig, and sits back down,
with all her ruling knives and forks intact.

The Two-Hundred-Pound
Potato Chip

When I put my hand in the wax
bag, often I pick out myself.

Wishing for something light and small
to go with a bottle of beer, ·

garnish the edge of my plate,
at this weight, I am the plate,

the table, a chip off...
my father said, Maine's pride.

Vocationally speaking, I gave up
the thought of undercover work,

too much night duty and always
having to look like you aren't there,

wearing what they wear, using
their ridged and salty accent,

walking a safe number of steps behind.
If I had my choice, I would settle

at the bottom of the local library
working my way through the oversized

and M's. But you know the rules,
no eating in the stacks, no talking,

there where my first order
of business is always to check out

who's skimming her text, twirling
her hair, blasé in the face

of the printed page. Who, after
the last technical phrase,

is beginning to feel that little
edge of hunger one or two chips

could ease, let alone what
a handful could erase.

The Hand of Peace

In the fifties, on the first early morning
talk show hosted by Dave Garroway, who has since
died by his own hand, the Kellogg company
sponsored a contest for cats and dogs
their owners claimed could talk. A panel
of judges, speech therapists and lexicographers,
listened to the howls and whines, the growling
barks and meows, and judged which sounds
were closest to human speech. Each pet
spent a minute making the most of his voice,
and his master was paid increasing amounts
for any noise that turned into a syllable
and then a word. A boxer from Indianapolis,
loyal to her time, sang the name
Eisenhower so well the General himself
invited her to the White House and later
took the dog on his campaign. Across
the country, pet owners were mouthing two-
and three-syllable words in front of their pets,
except the parakeet and myna bird, disqualified
because of their skill to mimic real talk.
A Vermonter thought of bringing in
a Canada goose that kept flying over her
in the nineteen fifties, who flew in a flock
that looked more like a tuning fork than a V.
Each time he honked he barked the words

Look. Look. Even if she could have
caught him, it's unclear how he would
have done sitting on the spot under
those hot studio lights. Dave Garroway sat
there for twenty years and signed off
each show with his hand held up
Indian-style, which today, flying over,
the geese still look for as a sign of *Peace*.

There

It's been too many years since we lived in Buffalo
with the War, and even the past cannot recall
all it has forgotten. I remember someone wrote
a number on my wrist as we walked down
Elmwood Avenue toward a demonstration against
George Wallace, who hadn't been shot yet. He said
to call it when we got busted and by the way
he had good acid. Then I didn't know what he meant
by "acid" and was only beginning to know I
could use my body by putting it in a place
the government objected to. I don't want to make
myself seem innocent or radical. I wasn't.
I was scared and confused. But when a Buffalo tactical
policeman pushed us with his nightstick
to keep us neatly on a sidewalk outside
the Hilton where Wallace was freely speaking,
I felt my body stiffen and can still feel it
to this day. One of the phrases we heard in the sixties
and saw written with Magic Marker was NO MORE
BUSINESS AS USUAL. So much business now,
fifteen years later, takes place at the keyboard,
especially the soft clicking keyboard of
the painless computer on which, it is said,
we "punch in" a program that can start the movement
of canned goods or warheads impossible to call
back. Now, when I dial Information to try
to find you again, I hear the fast-circuit

talk of a machine searching its made-mind
for the right combination of letters and numbers,
the code that means you still live someplace
familiar and can be reached when you are there.

In January Everything
That Can Break
Breaks Down

The small engines of our life
together quit.
When I try to draw water
from the tap and nothing
happens and you flip
a switch only to engage
the knowledge of what
you take for granted,
we look at each other
and say, *In January*
everything that can break
breaks down.
Janus bore two faces
to see his wife
both ways and sat
unadorned at the door
of heaven with no switch
to turn on or off.
Here, in our broken
heaven, I don't think
there hums a machine
of ours we couldn't
live without. Today
when all our two-faced
machines break down
and each repairman
we call is out until
next year, I think we

can make things work
if, as they say,
we put our heads together.
First rather,
let's start repairing
where we turn our faces
in to touch. Let's crank
the little horsepower
from our lips.

If You Asked

I can't say for sure she and I won't
touch, that a few bars from a song
hanging in the air might not be
enough to change what we thought
into what we did. That sounds too

country and western, but sometimes
those young bar singers saw what
they sang sitting night after night
in front of them and had to say it
outright to keep from taking it back

home to their rented rooms. I think
if I mouth their words, even when
we're kept close apart by the chords
of a slow dance, there still will be
time to think past what it might

feel like now. Thinking how I would feel
later is one way. Or what I would say
if you asked. I heard Hank Williams
had a bad back and sang from that pain,
too, as well as how he knew we get lost

when we touch and when we think not to.
He tied words to knot below the skin,
half because on hard nights he was strapped
into his guitar to keep him standing.
He knew what he had to lose.

I don't want to do anything to lose you,
even if you don't pick to ask. What I'm
not sure of yet is how to unsing a kiss
and, kissing you, strum out what I didn't
have the heart to do.

Dancing at Bread Loaf

I

Snow will drift over these porches,
and Cherry, Birch, and Maple,
dormitories of summer, write out
their shadows across the covered fields.
Yellow boards of the buildings
will appear gold against the snow.
If we watch from our August windows
while we stay here now,
we won't pass by in March,
mistaking this place for an abandoned inn.
At the Little Theater we'll need
to pull off our gloves and scrape the frost
from a small pane, in order to see
the stacked and folded chairs, the empty stage.
By then the great hall will be a closed
heave in the wind, a cooling oven,
and the pond, frozen over, nowhere to be seen.
Skiers can draft their lines across
the drifting fields, breaking the surface
of the snow, their steady poling taking
them out of sight. The winter moon will fix
its stars from falling. But sitting out tonight
after the last reading and dance,
preparing to go back tomorrow to our separate

cities, we can see the ecstatic summer
stars, falling and erasing themselves
from this page of the universe.

2

At tonight's good-bye dance,
I turn into a husband and touch
you in the thin agreement of dancing.
Caring for yourself, you ask about my wife,
so we are a pair of three, touching
and not touching in the perfect pulse
of the electric bass, the wavering flow
of the steel guitar. Here the moon is
the mountain's eye and the white noise
of crickets the steady sound of overhearing.
When the music is over,
the borrowed voice of the singer returned,
we are left alone to decide what to do
with our hands and lips.
Later, in the star-chilled air,
the pins of stars hold the punctuated
sky, and I can look up and see her asleep
in our married, half-empty bed, turning
in the early morning dream of good-bye.

3

Between dances, sitting with you by the face
of this fire, looking through the amber eyes
of the owl andirons, I remember
the first time I came here, seventeen.

My father took the wrong turn off
Route 7, thinking this was the college
he wanted me to see. A brook running west,
going the wrong way, ran beside the road.
Writers rocked on the porches,
convalescing I thought, although the books
they held made this look more like a school.
None of them was remotely my age,
and the buildings named for the nearby
trees were unlikely dormitories.
I had no way to imagine myself staying,
and told my father to turn around
without stopping. He had the presence
of mind to stop and ask where we were.
Telling you, I still try to turn
one of them into Frost, who may have been
there or near enough so I can say he was.
A year later, enrolled in the real college
in town, before classes began, I hiked
with the other freshmen to Frost's cabin.
Homesick and missing my city, I didn't see
his three apple trees giving their fruit
to the ground or the stone wall running
down the right side of the hay field.
I didn't hear the nuthatch and chickadee,
the underswell of crickets and breeze,
or feel darkness shining in the woods.
The first stars were giving themselves
away, and it was all I could do not to
go with them, now not to go with you.
Later that night at the student dance
in the Barn, I fell in love. Whenever

I return and meet you in this place
and we have not decided what our words mean
or where to take them, I can't tell
the difference between history and geography,
the difference between words that move me
or if you made them move across the night sky.

4

Once, far from here, drifting over
the divided streets of my city, I
heard two trumpets and a saxophone,
a liquid lead guitar, a drum delivering
its pulse and a singer bending the blues
away from his listeners. I went in,
too scared not to, and stood listening
to the four-bar chorus.
Everyone there was Black. I didn't
notice my mistake going in
was forgiven without asking for forgiveness.
Or that choosing, even by chance, to be alone
in the presence of others, a place by the bar
on which to stand. How easily I might
have been asked to leave or worse,
but that was only my thought, and no one
said anything except *good night and good-bye*.
I know there are places in your city
we aren't supposed to go, bars where we
could dance all night and forget our last names.
Here whenever I listen to music and want
to go one step further by dancing,
especially at the foot of this mountain

inside the Barn, I make sure I have brought
myself. And, after the band gives away its songs,
out among the pulsing stars, you invite me
to go home to the comfort of my own loneliness.

5

Today with no readings or workshops to attend,
we could have taken a path into the woods
behind Frost's cabin and walked through
a cathedral of pines. Or the other way,
east, halfway up Worth Mountain, we might have
climbed to the abandoned ski jump and hiked
to the crater lake of Lake Pleiad
to swim, even with the rumor of leeches,
then slept out under a hiker's lean-to.
Across from the Inn beyond the mown
meadow, West-Running Brook goes
as Frost's poem says it does. If we had asked,
a caretaker would have given us keys to the Printer's
Cabin or Tea House. Both have stone fireplaces
and the ashes of their own stories.
Behind Treman, there is a good sitting stone,
too large to have been moved by hand or team.
Sitting there we would have heard bumblebees
combing the farms of goldenrod around us,
and known how strange it is not to be noticed
this well. A half mile past Frothingham,
through the stone gates on the left,
we could have found a field of blueberries.
Other couples have returned with full baskets
and traces of blueberry on their lips

and hands. Tonight, sitting out, talking
about the places we might have gone,
we are bound to see the falling stars,
the constellation traced in the letters
of our first names.

6

Dozing at this dawn hour, you say
on rare occasions a bird is assigned
the name of the person who first saw it,
like Richardson's owl, the earless one.
The trees, cherry, birch, and maple,
carry their sound in the wind,
and, at first, have no other
meaning in our minds. When a mountain
suggests the perfect mystery of asking
nothing from us, we conceive it
in other terms, trying, the expression
goes, to bring it down to earth.
Here the mountains are no green mystery.
Yet in August the days bask in
themselves and the nights shiver.
Behind the Barn, past the pond,
that mountain disappears in the presence
of its mist, and appears to drift
off its mooring when the sun flaps
across the woods. After the last word
is spoken for this summer's conference,
staying up all night dancing and
following the stars,
we can enter the flour of dawn

and breathe in the scent of rising
bread, drifting down this distant morning
where, sleepless and falling
awake, we are still preparing to go.

Falling Awake

When I was drowsy and they were
trying to put me to bed,
mother and father would fly
to the words of their childhood,
as if I had disappeared, and they
were alone in their room,
the door ajar, their syllables
of immigration
marrying them again. Sometimes
now, even when I am not
tired, feeling two puffs
of their familiar breeze,
gai schlafen, gai schlafen,
go to sleep, I begin falling,
today under the branches
of the box elder, a bluebird
has landed for the first time,
in among the thick leaves,
so hidden I am not sure
this jewel rests there.
How can I love what I cannot see,
what I was taught not to love
this much, as if it were the same
sex as me, our feathers ruffling
together? Where is the ribbed leaf
carrying the lovely word *faigeleh*
some use to mean fag,
mother first meant to say
little bird, perhaps bluebird,
perhaps this one?

Prayer for My Son
Asleep with His Sword

Now is your time for swords,
knives, daggers, a sharp word

and, this year, a bright cosmic
light saber called THE FORCE.

When you cry out
in your sleep, I come in

and pull up the covers you've kicked
off. You must feel something

change, because you smile under
the sleep of your eyes

and reach behind you to find
the plastic handle of your knife.

There will always be a sword
sticking in a stone, looking for

its true name, waiting to be
wakened from its cold dream.

Yours, Sam, is another word
for Arthur and the syllables

I see on your lips that say
the Jedi name Luke Skywalker.

When the cold comes inside
your covers, may you hold

the hand of your dream.
When a stone stops singing

the story of its king,
may you lend it your sword.

When you roll over and feel
nothing beside you,

may all my mays
and *The Force Be with You.*

The Two of Us

Out walking, holding hands, you say,
Look, our shadows make an M.
I wasn't thinking how we start

to write ourselves across the snow
until the sun changes or one
of us decides to let go. But for you

at three, the world beside our house
spells itself into alphabets
that start with A or M. I've been

meaning to show you how some things
work— the grosbeak's bill is forged
into a V in order to split a sunflower

seed, and the brook below our field
only looks like one because we've had
a January thaw. For a minute

I've forgotten you're not two
and not asking why all the time,
although I bless you now for how you've

made me look more closely, even at
a sparrow's nest near the roof's peak
that threatens to clog a vent

and will put me higher than I like
to climb on our extension ladder.
Letting go and running ahead, your

arms and legs fly through the letters
of the alphabet like a sailor flagging
through his semaphore. I do see some

of the words your red and blue snowsuit
spells and, when you fall, the shape
of the angel that lies there under you.

Away from Us

When we say good-bye now,
it's most likely for good.

Not that we are dying, although
death, too, earns its diploma

and loves us as well as grandmother
and grandfather. Today,

when we march in, we are still
held together by chalk dust

and the quickly scrawled
PLEASE SAVE. DO NOT ERASE.

I know I am not your father,
and yet as Roethke, another

teacher, wrote, "with no rights
in this matter," I say

these fathering words that will
take you further than you want

to go. I sense you want me to meet
your father, though we will have

nothing long to say. For him
to have shared you leaves us

speechless, wanting the list
of names and honors to go on

forever, because when you
march out, tasseled and smiling tears,

you walk away from us both.

Reading at Night

The words on this page
cannot raise the sound
of your voice until
I read them, silently
move my lips in the cadence
of their syllables.
When a breeze slips into
the room, it turns another
page, lifts a letter
on the night table, taking
your signature back
to the leafless elms.
My breath doesn't sound
like the wind, but sometimes
at night, when I step outside
of myself and lean down,
I hear the little air
escape like a breeze and slip
back into my paper body.
I need you to stand
over me then and move your lips,
until the words you are
reading revive the speechless
air and I can slide under
the one slow sound of your voice
back into the page
of my body.

How We Know We're Here
for Cornwall in Celebration of
the Two-Hundredth Turning of Her Tine

When the fields are braided in windrows
and the cough of the kick baler
kicks another bale into the dry air

when apple blossoms bring the bees
out of the boxed cities of their hives
and the trees hum with their safe gathering

when rain washes a thin film of spray
from the apples' skins and the orchard
air sings and drones in the engine-strained
dives of the sprayer's deeds

when the sun edges the Green Mountains
and on the other side of day
the Adirondacks and all shades of known
light take place in the shimmer
and hay-scent of this mown valley

when elm, birch, and maple are signaled
again from something far and close inside
and signal us by turning each leaf on,
each leaf and pine needle back to the ground

when deer still run down between
the swamp and orchards and can be seen
before they are taken down or bound away

when first snow begins to fill in
the fields, turning a key in the town
shed that starts the powerful and painful
happy heave of the town plow

when the lights blow and power lines
loop from pole to pole and outside
only the wind is speaking
in swirls, trying to get away from itself
in the smoky puff of a downdraft

when the snow settles and someone steps
out on the unbroken road on their skis
or newly tuned snow machine and sets
a track the next snow will erase

when the air barely warms enough
to draw the frost out and sap up
and the known mud of the road is tracked
into the added-on mudroom

when finally the ground is bare and soft
enough not to break a shovel tip
we need to turn our Cornwall clay
back into useable earth

and digging down we hit the long store
of broken tractor pieces and bottle bits
clinging to the clay like burdock to a sock

and they are still held by some of our last names—
Abernathy, Robbins, Bingham, Sperry, Peet,
and Foote—to which we now add ours, turning
on the tine of our two-hundredth year.
It's how we know we're here.

from *Fire in the Orchard* (2002)

Dead Creek

I wasn't there for them
  but for the slow brown water

drifting me by the newly
  plowed fields and the perching

hawks, taking me into
  a cove of lilies and cattails,

no faster than the breeze not even
  riffling into waves, carrying me

like a leaf into shallow water
  where someone had built a box

on an iron pole and a banded
  Canada goose was sitting her

eggs until I came close enough
  so she would have to lift off,

leaving me to read the numbers
  around her neck, like a survivor's wrist,

leaving me to remember I wasn't there
  for the teenager drinking wine

in the parking lot I had left behind
  for the water, nor for the denim

man, older than her father, who was
   pressing her against his truck, not

against her will, and touching her
   crotch in the bright daylight before

noon, before I began paddling,
   drawing the water toward me.

Road Lulav

Here God is a weed
    sticking out of the ditch.
And I am the only Jew
    around to see him.

The tall, four-leaved stalk
    brushes the nearby hay
and the dust a car raises
    fishtailing over this hill.

I didn't know I needed
    a sprig of God
until I saw it
    and thought of that

lovely pair, lulav
    and esrog—palm leaf
and lemon—the rabbi
    would bring into the house

of the temple.
    I suppose the wind speaks
Hebrew too, so any prayer
    I remember would not be

lost if I said it,
    even if what I say is
by heart, the precise meaning
    of the words lost to me.

Once my mother said
   I grew like a weed,
she couldn't keep me in clothes.
   There's no shirt she could

sew for this road weed,
   if she were here, if God
told her to come back
   with her needle and thread.

The Burning Bush of Basketball

It's just God dressed up as Michael Jordan.
Larry Bird, 1986

He was everywhere at once—
   driving past Bird and dunking,
stepping into three-point land
   and hitting nothing but net,
bulling into the lane in traffic
   and hooking up what some call
garbage. Nearly everything
   he shot went in, from almost
anywhere on the court. And high
   above courtside, even Johnny
Most, the voice of the Celtics—
   none more biased than he—
with his voice-box of gravel,
   sang praises, sang praises.
Nothing worked to stop him—
   double-teams or triple-teams,
not the illegal zone defense,
   for which they were warned and hit
with a technical. The wall of
   Parish, Walton, and McHale
he went through or around.
   And the smooth, defensive glove
of Johnson he took off.
   And the pesky, adolescent rage
of Ainge he blessed with a smile
   and a hoop. The great Bird,

with all of his blond points,
    played as if he were watching,
as if the basket and basketball
    combined into a burning bush,
all fire, all voice. Everyone
    inside the Garden, and at home
outside the Garden, watched what
    no one had ever done before.
Jordan went to the well of the basket
    and drew up bucket after bucket
of which the final number 63
    was added to his playoff name
in the line score, in the team totals
    (still not enough to win)
for which we sang praise that Sunday
    God was a bull from Chicago, winning
us over, burning the parquet floor.

Night Call to You and the Wind
of Chernobyl

No one can say what the peepers say
   into the ears of the darkness. Sometimes
it's *Stay*. Tonight it's *Leave, leave*.

I know what it's like being away from home
   when the world takes an unexpected turn
from the wrong lane and there isn't a right

tree to climb and sing from. But I don't
   know how it is for you, over there,
where the air has suddenly been sprayed

with dust that sours the milk, unripens
   the fruit. Now it's up to the wind again,
the way it often is, after something invisible

and radiant has been put into the air.
   There are times when the wind turns around
on itself and the peepers I hear pulsing

below in the field disappear and can only
   sing to themselves. I wish I could say more
surely whether you should stay or leave.

I don't want any fiery breeze to touch
   your voice or anyone else's who likes to sing
back on a spring night to the tree frogs,

some of whom leave for the willow branches,
　　some of whom stay on the ground.
Warnings will speak to women and children.

And it is men like us who tremble too
　　and must take our trembling back
to the unmarried wind, back to our beds

we leave each night, for the songs
　　that cannot stay in the green throats
that sing them, that cannot extinguish the air.

Here, Pepi

Sit on my chest,
I call to this generous
chihuahua. And he jumps up
and lies close to my troubled
airway, absorbing whatever
the little well of his chest can.

I wish you might hear him
tell his own story,
but he is too busy wheezing,
having returned from today's
round of healing house calls,
decisive visitations.
The neighborhood's asthmatics
know whom to ask for,
when they can't breathe,
when there is no inhalant
near at hand.

The cured call Pepi their Jesus
dog, and even his picture
by the family crucifix
brings some relief.

I'm not one of them yet.
But sometimes this cough hangs on
or, God forbid, turns into pneumonia,
for which there is some medicine,
for which I wait for his chest
to stop heaving, so I, too, can rest
him close to my heart and say,
Here, Pepi, here.

The Boss's Son

I wanted to sit where the pin boys did,
   on the back ledge of the pit,
so I could see the brown eight-pound
   ball spinning toward the pins,
toward me. I wanted to push the shake-
   mop down each of the alleys, returning
the lanes to their lacquered shine.
   I died to run the elevator, like any
of your hired men, to try to bring the car even
   with a customer's requested floor,
praying you had not paid off the inspector
   not to check the cables that month,
that year. I wanted to brush down the slate
   pool tables, each covered
with its own green felt and, by the end
   of a day's play, dusty as a horse's blanket.
I wanted to close up, to count the bills
   and change, that day's receipts, and fill out
a slip with numbers to match the money
   in the till you would find when you went
to work in the morning, before I was
   awake, before my dream of setting pins,
of sending a ball back on its slow return.

A Shadow of a Nest

The Human Cannonball climbs down into
   the barrel of the cannon, safe in the tube's
darkness, waiting, like me, for the film to punch
   him up the metal shaft and into the canvas

air, down-tent, to the inflated landing bag.
   I'm holding my breath because a pair
of purple finches have nested in the exploding
   fuchsia next to the door and are gun-shy

when anyone comes or goes, so their young
   are fed more on my family's comings and
goings than their own hunger. Mother
   flits from the willow to the box elder,

waiting for evening, for a lull long enough
   to poke a seed into a new throat. So I
ask everyone to use the back door which is
   easy to forget to do and not to scent the nest

with our kind, out of curiosity or the wish
   to kiss a berry into one of the four blind
gaping mouths. Father, rosy and raspberry,
   not purple, stays on a near branch, as if

standing on a spring, waiting to see if I will
   have the courage to breathe, when the Human
Cannonball is launched into the air
   and turns himself like a maple leaf, a snow

goose feathering into a cornfield, toward
   the arms of the audience, which can never
take the place of the pink blown-up plastic
   bag that will save him a few frames and words

from now—if I can stand here, still as a shadow
   of a nest, breathing like the wind that flies
through the weedy branches of the box elder,
   here, empty as the air that needs to take him up.

Fire in the Orchard

As if autumn's own ripening weren't enough,
    or the pilot's instructive spray could bring the trees
to bear. As if the grass hadn't been mowed between
    rows to keep the weeds down, so a pruner

could cut away the dead branches. As if the pickers
    didn't twist the fruit off into their baskets and then
dump them into the orchard's crates, for a forklift to
    stack onto a flatbed and drive to the storage house.

As if some of the apples hadn't
    been missed or dropped, left for a doe to make
herself sick on or find under the snow in a month
    when there's nothing in sight to browse. As if

the fruit hadn't begun to turn and sugar, cider
    in its own skins, drawing the crazy yellow jackets
out. As if the apples weren't green hay
    in a barn or a pile of oily rags in a cellar, frayed

wires beginning to overheat, throw sparks. As if no
    one thought they couldn't burn in their own fermenting
fuel and no one knows yet what started the biggest
    blaze in Shoreham's life, a match or the trace of a stray

bullet from Ticonderoga. Or two apples filled with their
    own sweet proof, rubbing like sticks in their crate, until
they burst into flame, apple by apple, all seventy
    thousand bushels blazing up, exploding this red harvest.

In Audubon's Notebook

It's possible for birds to sew
    the air between two feeders,
one hanging in the box elder,
    the other in the elm. Finches
and sparrows flit to the end
    of their line and return, the way
moving the typewriter carriage used
    to bring a page up. They only know
they are feeding, although there seems
    to be an order, as to who lights first, someone
watching could record. They spill enough
    seed for a pair of cardinals to disturb
the snow, although it's too much
    to say they are the blood drops of a shot
dog drawn to beef fat nailed into
    the box elder's bark. The downy
woodpecker won't care who's underneath,
    when he comes to drill the grease.
Is it too much to say there isn't
    a poem that doesn't need to know how
the birds stitch the air? It's possible,
    when Audubon was sitting in a field,
he forgot to note what was there
    and wrote something that had nothing
to do with the purple tint of a wing.
    He didn't have the heart to write

he knew, in death, he would see
   his mother again, perhaps forever,
a fear not sewn into his body.
   That's what he couldn't bear to see,
so, instead, thought to look up and write,
   in his slanted hand, what later he would read—
The nuthatch has something stuck in
   his throat. Gray stone. Part song.

The Happy Net

We're in their nation,
    on their land, in their gym,
although with names like
    Chagnon, Trombley, and
Bourbeau in the lineup,
    you wouldn't know
Trombley's great-grand-
    father was Dark Cloud,
in the program's picture, a tall
    chief standing alone
and, apparently, unguarded.
    My daughter is matched
up against Chevalier, and
    their ponytails, blond and
black, are swishing
    the air, when they bang
bodies, when they reach
    for the ball that wants to
escape them. At halftime,
    after tonight's winning
lottery ticket is announced,
    Mr. Laroque, the power
forward's father, continues
    telling the story of the Happy
Net, in English, although there are
    a few words that slip through
in Abenaki and French. He says
    the net was once sewed so well
that outside, in the Missisquoi,
    new trout and bass would swim

into it with a cold smile, thinking
    they were still in the river.
Three fish, and his family would
    have one full stomach. Each of
our girls must have taken his story
    to heart, because, in the last
few minutes, they are hitting
    nothing but net, filling the basket.

Nothing Else We Had to Share

Ahead on the bridge a few
   men were fishing their lives
out of the Matanzas River.
   All they reeled in, in that span,
were whiting and blues, catfish
   and drum, and, some said, the love
of their bait and where their
   bait went. I stood next to
the only Black man I knew
   in that moment to talk about
nothing—his luck, the tides,
   his full freezer, his sons
and mine, who didn't eat fish.
   Good thing there was nothing
else we had to share, although
   who knows, in that sun and breeze,
at that height, what history
   would remember to forget, what
habit could be cast over the railing
   only to be reeled in empty.
Who knows if his line would come
   back knotted by a few rising leaves
it would take the two of us to untangle?

Shovel and Rake

Even in battle, crops and sacred objects must always be spared.
Mohammed

Praise to the prophet, I think, looking
   out on my wife's garden, her wavy
rows and beds of mulch.

Praise to this piece of yard she can
   bury her knees and dig her hands into.
Praise to the warrior who walks by her,

weeding, his spear dripping on the dirt
   road, who looks over her way,
in a way I believe he doesn't see her,

snapping peas and pulling up
   the dirty bulbs of the beets.
Who recognizes the way she has

leaned the shovel against the rake
   so they can be seen by anyone
returning with blood on his hands.

Who is looking over the old hay fields
   at the smoke, which is having its own trouble
rising and not praising her pepper's fire.

Fall Term

These burrs on the cedar branches are no
   bother. Neither are the curling black
willow leaves the frost tints yellow
   and brown. Before I know it, I can see
my way clear to the gray granite art
   building, where two students are toeing
in to its ragged stone edges, imagining,
   I think, they are on Everest and not a few
yards across from their new dormitory,
   where the spines of their books haven't
been broken yet or anything written
   on a clean sheet of paper. Because no leaf
ever went to college, when there was
   a breeze and the late afternoon sun came
to an open window, like the yellow jackets
   who know enough not to study and the blue
jays who never fail at anything.

To the Young Woman Looking
for an Eating Disorder Workshop
Who Found a Poetry Reading Instead

In any case, come in.
I know this isn't exactly what
you were looking for. It isn't

easy walking into a room
of strangers who look happy
enough and yet are waiting to be

fed. Sometimes I think of words
as food and yet, like you, must give
back what I take in—like the thought

I can hold a word in my mouth
to keep the world together,
to put food in those mouths

that appear nightly like gaping
sparrows. I wasn't going to say this
but, in my other life, I talk

with girls who starve themselves
or give up their food, in the hope
that talking—when it comes down

to it, two mouths giving and taking—
will let the world take care of itself
so those girls can begin feeding

themselves again, sitting at the table.
By now you may realize this is
no workshop to solve this, or, to use

the words, I'm afraid, on the tip
of my tongue, no fast-food solution.
I'm not sure your listening here

will change anything, sitting in between
the rows of these stanzas, but perhaps,
after the reading, before we both must

leave, we will have a chance
to say a few words to each other, our sweet
luck by which to remember this hour.

Civil Union and the Breeze
July 1, 2000

I should have known better
than to let my green
bird take a moment out
in the air. That the high
branches of the box elder
and birch and then
the maple and eventually
the poplar would be too
much for either of us.
It wasn't as if he wanted
to go anywhere else
except someplace breezy
and higher, where he
could still hear me
beseech him. From there
he could probably see
my children, a few states
away, both in their new
lives, and, below him,
cars, now that the law
was passed, lining up
at the town clerk's door,
so their drivers could
pay civilly for a civil
license, not to love,
which was already theirs,
but to live with some
of the rights of a bird
in Vermont's green breeze.

This Forever

How did darkness know how to show us
   that first time, *how and where,*

when the word of our bodies said,
   Now? You knew when to say *Here*

before I did, before I had anything
   to remember. Later, when it got light,

one of us didn't have to think to say,
   Again, because our bodies remembered

that first time there were no words
   and that nothing, this forever, lasts.

Reunion

The peonies are closed, not boiled
   Brussels sprouts, a bouquet of fists.
With an hour of sun, they'll come
   undone into their strong flop of
petals and drop everything about
   themselves underneath, onto
the ground. A few bees will think
   they can take something back

and will fly all day in their scent—
   sweet waste that doesn't stick to
their wings, their legs. I'm back
   among the fallen, dazed, having
walked into the past at this dinner
   dance. There's someone old to love
again and a boy I knew who didn't die
   in a paddy. Another stands alone, open

as a hand and newly sober. I saw
   him changing in his truck before
he came in. It wouldn't take much
   for us to sit in rows and put
our heads down on our desks,
   and now to say the words
you once kept inside, I'm pleased you said.
   Even those flowers, hard buds first,

fall apart into their blossoms,
    too heavy for their stems.
It's late enough to stay a few more
    minutes. The wind will sweep petals
up against the house, against that
    other wall that holds too many names in
gold, that pulls us back to stand in front of it
    whenever we think it's time to go.

from *Below the Falls* (2010)

State of My Nation Address

Neighbors and chickadees,
colleagues and compatriots,
citizens of the world, elves
and newts,

today I am not standing before you.
No one has required me to give
my accounting of the past year.

I am one of the unelected
sitting by a window filled
with the bounty
of grief.

I have no more to say
about the economy
than the sauce that remains
on my lips from yesterday.

And nothing new to add to
our progress in the war
though it appears few of us
can remember when it began.

Allow me to start over,
to pledge my allegiance to the flag
that hasn't been sewn yet,
that none of us will feel
compelled to stand for.

Before I forget I want to thank
my wife and my lover,
the bluebird, who is queen
of distractions.

Before I forget I want to salute
all veterans of foreign wars.

Nothing is foreign to me anymore
and I wish I could shake each
of your hands.
My assistant, the field, tells me

you are no less than these blades
of grass, leaves who served
our country.

This is the point where I am
expected to make promises.

I promise to weep with you.
I promise to stand in line.
I promise to share my recipe
for a thin sauce made of paper
and limes,
something that might appeal
to both sides of an aisle.

Did I forget to mention God?
I hope not. I hope some god
I haven't met yet is being
invented instead of another

government.
I've instructed my aide-de-camp
to lie in waiting for the arrival
of a little spirit,

esprite-de-corps.
To let me know when I've remembered
to say everything I needed
about the hope of the wind.
When my time is up,
when that red flag inside the meter
clicks down, telling me time has
expired.

What We Thought We Said and Saw

for Mickey Heinecken

I can't say what images
    in a poem mean to anybody else
but you, coach, or what we'll think
    to say later about the herds of deer
we saw dead on the road on our ride
    to the championship game. We talked
all the way down and back about
    everything else, almost—work, wives
and what it would take for our team
    to win in that stadium that couldn't
hold a deer. Men's talk, I suppose.
    The Lakota say *Mitakuye Oyasin*—
We are all related—whenever they see
    a dead relation on the path.
We would have been singing
    that song all the way to Piscataway,
New Jersey, given all we saw
    on the shoulders, in the medians.
I wanted to stop and carry a few
    of the most damaged ones back
into the woods. But before I thought
    to say so, the urge was gone.
And there were stores where the trees were.
    It's amazing, too, how quickly
a winning score can erase a kill count.
    (Our school did win.) Amazing
what we thought we said and saw.

Shout-out

There are a million invisible
    muscles I never took the time
to thank. I thought they would
    think my gratitude lame.

Neither did I stop to praise
    my nerves, which sometimes
went without saying, didn't shout.
    Nor my bones, those hangers

I hung the shirt and pants
    of my flesh on. I was very
surprised when my eyes
    began seeing things I wasn't

looking at, like veracity
    and the grateful vireo.
I'm hard-pressed not to forget
    how my blood flowed

without my knowing it,
    and all its tributaries to whom
I failed to pay tribute.
    I'm not on death row. No one's

making a cross over me.
    My tongue deserves
a closet acknowledgment.
    And, before I forget, a big

shout-out to my nails
   Ripley asked me to believe
would go on forever
   without me.

The Missing

I'm missing someone
  I don't know, who isn't
where he's supposed to be.
  How do you find someone

who isn't there, who isn't
  answering? He could have
wandered off, before anyone
  knew he was gone. Everyone's

hoping he's not what the snow
  is for. Snow doesn't become
him, can't comb his hair.
  He didn't take his coat.

No one can wear a coat
  of ice very long. He's a son
and friend, our school's student.
  When a boy is gone,

no matter how old he is,
  he becomes my son. Can he
find a way to be found?
  That's what the ground is for.

To give back what it can't hold,
  to miss what it held, a boy gone
cold. There's a prayer that tries
  to call who's missing.

Somewhere there's a god
    for this, who answers in
a voice of ice and snow,
    we don't know when to expect.

Snow Day

I slide backwards
   down a hill I can't drive up.
I could walk to work
   if I had a week. I could
love staying home.
   I don't own a plow. I have
a shovel and my hands.
   I have to choose
to love everything I see
   in reverse—the field
under the snow,
   my wife waving to me
next to her car in the ditch.
   I wish I could stop for her.
I wish life wasn't a road of ice
   underneath the snow.
I wave a promise I'll come
   back, as I slide by.
I shouldn't be thinking
   about the stream below,
a neighbor named
   Beaver Brook.
Brooks are the first streams
   trickling off the hill when
the snow slips into drive.
   They show the beavers
it's time for spring. I wouldn't
   call this snow a problem,

here in Vermont. The children
    pray for a day off from school
they have to make up at the end
    of the year. Too much snow
will have them sitting at
    their desks next summer,
looking back at today,
    making up for what was lost.
It won't cost me anything
    to stay home with my children
who are grown and found their ways
    into the unplowed world.
I can spend all day shoveling
    with my wife who finds
her way back to our house.
    We could shovel the whole field,
if we had another day
    saved to stay home.

After the Fact
for Kymberlea L. Durant

I heard you say
the Army tries to turn
its women into men,
makes them hard for war.

You said to make you feel
low a man above you,
and women who had been
made into men, would call you

female. You weren't allowed
to wear anything under your
clothes you used to wear,
nothing soft or private.

Single girls were called
whores and ordered to undress,
to see if they were wearing
anything soft and private.

You weren't sure you wanted
to enlist. You'd been
a wild girl and said you needed
an army's discipline.

You couldn't know things
would come to this.
Driving home, I listened
to the radio. I heard you

say you were raped, taken
in a barracks next to yours,
and couldn't tell anyone who
loved you, not your mother

or your father. You were ready
to make a rank above you
and needed to send money home,
trained not to question

orders. I wanted to pull off the road,
enlist anyone who would listen
to me say that, in my work,
I talk with women and men

who have been raped, who are afraid
no one will believe them. Taken
by a friend turned enemy, with no
obvious war between them.

I wanted to let you know
I heard you. I have a civil
daughter and a civilian son.
All sons need to know what it means

when a soldier says *No*.
You say you've talked your niece out
of enlisting, a girl, like you,
filled with promise. I want

to promise you I won't forget,
I won't stop listening to anything
you have to say, you can
tell me on the radio.

Dylan in Vermont

I can just afford this seat
   in the grandstand. With so many
rows between us, I have to

believe you are there,
   by what I hear, by knowing
you are singing under your wide-

brimmed hat, reminding me
   of those other years,
the other war. Isn't that

why I'm here? Trying
   to remember a picture
of you, young, as you still sound,

under our amplified sky.
   I'm not hoping this is
a high school reunion.

But isn't it true that's where
   we go to find someone we lost,
we loved, who remembers us?

The kid behind me is smoking
   a sweet grass like the mown hay
lying in the fields

beyond the fairgrounds. All
   I'm handing down are my strong
glasses, so anyone in my row

can see who she is hearing.
   I don't expect you'll say hello
between songs. You never did.

That's for us to do, among
   ourselves. That's what
the mountains are for

tonight, to sing back
   what they hear
at any cost.

Before the Election

I cast one vote
for the snow, caucus

of one. I don't live
in New Hampshire.

The snow can win,
if a canvasser knocks

on its door to get
the vote out.

I love the snow more
than my country.

My lawyer says
it's a reasonable treason.

I used to live near
the Caucasus Mountains

and eat couscous
before the election.

The great state of
blizzards casts one vote

for the next president,
for the vice-president

of plows. I hope
I'll be snowed in

and nobody can reach
my door with a pamphlet.

I hate being leafleted.
The teacher-in-me is praying

for a snow day. I'm not
an anarchist, I know.

I still pray. I love the notion
of a nation. The plow roars

like a tank in the middle
of the night. I don't want to

forget the white field,
blank as a canvas.

For Hospice Volunteers

What do you say to the living
   who are dying, who look out
to the orange day lilies?

   What can they hear of
any flower, wild or not, blooming
   in a ditch, opening in a vase

for more than a day?
   Maybe nothing. Maybe nothing
more than anyone knows where

   a petal goes, after it's gone
into the ground, after I try
   remembering that fragrance

I felt like a breeze, by the side of the road,
   waving without saying so,
when both of us knew you were leaving.

Conjugating March

A Roman, who didn't live
   in Vermont, named this month
for what he didn't know.
   A Centurion wouldn't want to

march in snow for a month.
   Here in Middlebury, we're
in the middle of mud season,
   meaning, in this town,

by the green, we know to nod
   and walk by each other on the street
when we feel the urge, like a sword,
   to say something mean

and mean it. We've had enough
   of thinking April's spring,
enough of being on the verge.
   Even the memory of Dud Phinney,

our local pro, hitting his seven
   iron from green to green amidst
the snow, isn't enough for us to pray
   any harder for what we can't make

happen faster than the sap marching,
   camping in a cold tree at night.
March is for sharpening swords
   and practicing our swings,

for conjugating *march* in Latin,
   for keeping to ourselves and
muttering, for cursing the snow
   still left to plow.

Raising a Banner in the Garden

God needs to gaze into the rafters,
to look up to the past, to see His Name
that has become a number.

Remember Jungle Jim Loscutoff,
a box of a man, whose name, not number,
boxes out the sun, elbows the moon?
He hangs there because he won.

And Togo Palazzi who shot
with both hands, memory raises
above the parquet floor?

God knows our names go up
in smoke. Red Auerbach can't
come back, but the drift
of smoke can, at the end of a game.

Even God needs a ring before
He retires, something gold
and green for the afterlife—

not a bird, but piercing
our hearts like a ray,
a fierce gem, a garnet.

Young Man with the Unwanted Thought

You were shaking, telling me
   you didn't know where it came from.
You hadn't been feeling blue,

so it seemed to come out of the blue.
   You never thought this about
yourself before. No man had tried

to love, to touch you,
   you knew of. You'd never
fallen asleep and dreamt

of a man with the same feeling
   you have for the wind turning
the windmill, the snow in March

that doesn't know how to leave.
   Nothing I'd say could console you,
not the thought of love

coming out of the blue.
   Nor could I take your
shaking into me, as I have

the snow and the wind.
   *Sometimes you can love
your fear*, I wanted to say.

Remember the Shakers,
    who danced into
ecstasy when they loved someone

they couldn't touch, someone
    they didn't know was God,
a man, a woman, a turning

blade in the wind?
    Even God can't be consoled
when we won't love

who there is to love.
    I can't tell if I'm shaking
or dancing, when I'm out-

side in the snowy wind,
    when there's nothing more to
love than the thought of you.

A Tide Is Hard to Please

My children will sit
  in a tide, knee-high,
when they're at work
  by the ocean side.
They won't wear shoes
  to work. They'll roll their
pants up to their knees.
  I hoped to cool the Earth
before I died. A tide is
  hard to please. Have you
ever heard of the Earth
  going cold-turkey?
That would be a cool
  thing to imagine. What
if I never died? My
  children wouldn't have
to cry. They wouldn't break
  open a cloud. I used to
be proud of my Earth
  until it died. I used to
walk by the water
  with my pants rolled up.
It's hard not to imagine
  dying, being dead.
I love this earth
  as much as the breath
of my children.
  At work they'll want
to look at a cloud and think
  it's me, and not their shoes
floating next to their beds.

Snow and Ash
after Childe Hassam's
Boston Common at Twilight

I like to think of you
as the woman from another
century, walking with her

daughters beside the Common
at twilight in winter, sprinkling
bread for the pigeons who have

come out of the shadows,
a burnt snow. Because a fire
behind the buildings

illuminates the bare trees
with its rose light, its common god.
I like to think of you as the gas lamps

coming on. Because, with what is
burning out of control a few streets away—
these carriages and streetcars,

that sidewalk, its crowd of topcoats,
its line of men—will need more light,
so they can make their way home.

So a painter nearby can feel
the mood a mother with her two daughters,
especially the one casting bread,

want to express, for all time.
So he can render a calm
inside a panicky sky. Can

imagine me thinking of you
each time I come to his snow,
an ash the birds can eat.

Walking across the Fairway

for Robert Jimerson

We could have thought
   that still white spot
was a ball, lost in the rough

at the edge of the woods—
   a Top-Flite, a Pinnacle,
the coveted Nike.

Could have thought
   it was the tail of a deer
signaling truce, welcoming

surrender. And not really
   the red fox,
with his white-tipped tail,

walking across the fairway,
   striding like a tiger
or someone who knows

he can lie down,
   where mice burrow
in the hazards.

And how close he can let
   a pair like us come,
before he would realize

we aren't what he is,
   aren't meant for the woods,
unless we are lost, searching

for what we had hit a moment
   ago and now the last
twosome of the day.

Foreclosure

I have to sell my house back
to God. The mice can't afford it.

I'm all for mortgages
I can't afford until

I can't afford it. My mice
won't sleep on the street. Wall

Street is the house nobody shares.
I wish I had more interest

in Wall Street and my house
with God's name on it.

I wish America, my house,
shared and didn't borrow

its name from an Italian
mouse. I want to call my banker

a louse, of course, but he shared
it was my job to read the small print.

I've never lived in a tent before.
What's a street for?

I've never washed in a stream
and not used hand cream.

My hood in the suburbs used to
be a neighborhood. I used

to think God was superb,
the Extreme Good. I used

to pray I could live in His House.
I never thought I would hear

a rapper in my ear rap
on my tent. I never thought

paper money would be
no good. When I die,

put coins on my eyes.
Keep my lids closed.

I don't want to stare at anyone.
I did everything I could.

Below the Falls

Those rainbow-colored plastic
  boats bobbing below the falls
weave between a line

  of slalom poles.
Otter Creek is white,
  high enough to make

this course, their run, Olympic.
  Those kayakers aren't
looking just to make it

  through. They're looking, no,
fishing, for a boy who should be
  in his courses and not

fallen into this failing
  water. They have to keep
from getting tangled

  in the jam of winter logs
they hope to find him in.
  Hoping, too,

not to find anyone
  who shouldn't be found
there. It looks like half

the town is leaning over
the bridge to see what they'll
    come up with. Often a few

tourists would be taking
    pictures. The spray
makes rainbows

    when it isn't raining.
Usually we'd have
    something else to do.

But this boy is lost, born to be
    our winter son. The only gold
to be won is to see him

    swimming in
a wet suit among the boaters,
    or standing on

the thawing bank, throwing
    out a line, an oar,
another boy can reach.

Happy New Year 3008

The ball in Times Square
   will fall a hundred times,

Dick Clark shine
   in the night sky.

We'll elect our first transsexual
   president and hope

we won't need to row from
   our house

to a dock at the North Pole,
   walk on stones floating up.

And the last war for
   oil will be an asterisk like

the history of baseball. No one
   will speak of a lost generation.

A pill will thrive on
   its own side-effects.

We'll be able to plant trees
   in the desert of our handhelds,

be commended for *Giving Back*
   to the environment.

Grief will be a fruit of the past,
  its basket a new hat.

Another god will be found
  and deleted without remorse.

And you'll remember the story
  of your great-uncle, regretting

a century of universes
  you could feel in your heart,

when a battery runs down.
  When a rose fades

on a screen, when standing
  in the Square, looking up,

I turn to you for what was
  called a *kiss*.

His Own Ground

His body's found,
   what the river drowned.
Believe his mother is

   relieved. The town wants
to find she has her relief.
   Ice isn't very nice,

above the ground.
   His body can't say
if he wanted to slip.

   Results are slippery.
His mother takes him
   to his own ground.

Most of us live
   near a river
we don't own,

   we can walk to
outside of town.
   Students are sent

away, so they can be
   on their own,
not so a river can

fill with grief.
No one can say
   if he stepped into

the water to pray,
   if he stayed there
beyond anyone's faith.

   Ice isn't made to hold
anyone this long,
   to sing his unfound song.

Praise for *Raking the Winter Leaves:*

Raking the Winter Leaves is the work of a poet with a gift for meditative attention, falling awake in our precarious century, where "war never says one thing/ and means another." In a New England of town meetings, harvests, hay-scent, bee hum, and a sprig of God, Margolis reminds us that that "something was said here once to wake up/ a nation." Over three decades, this poet's lyric art has held calm vigilance, alert to things as precise as a cow's numbered ear, her "black and white/map of a head." As wars end and begin in the war president's "gobbling song," still much can yet be seen in in the "branchless/ forest of the clouds."

Margolis writes as a husband, father, counselor, healer, and citizen of the Republic, where, he confesses, "Doubt/is my democracy." His language is light and tensile, playful and sprung from its own music, where we are never far from such hard-won admissions as conclude a poem on the art of dying, where, he writes "I have done everything I could." For having done that and more, abundant gratitude."

—Carolyn Forché
Blue Hour

I hope this sweep over a lifetime of words will show the world that Gary Margolis is a distinctively American poet to be celebrated and honored as one of the classics. At times he reminds you of his neighbor Frost, at his best, though Gary is more contemporary and dimensional. He does the poet's thing of turning the ordinary into a revelatory text on the meaning of things. Like a Vermont pond in the sunshine, every poem emits layer upon layer of light, helping us to see what we usually overlook or simply don't have the eyes to notice.

—Thomas Moore
Care of the Soul and *A Religion of One's Own*

For over three decades now, Gary Margolis has been refining his considerable virtues: among them a steady, Horatian speaking voice—wry, lucid, affecting. These are remarkably attentive poems, combining astute observation of experience with a capacity for listening that is a rare thing when the period style seems to call for chest-thumping posturing. As he tells us in a searching elegy for a fellow poet, "Oh, for the life grief gives./A prescription for grieving/And side effects we can live/With, like living…

—David Wojahn
World Tree

Like a cop or a reporter, Gary Margolis works a beat, at once his little patch of New England and "the whole wide world." It would be easy to regard him as a poet of place, and surely he is, for his poems take us places, often more than one at a time: a country road and the barricades of a protest; an undulating sea and Fenway Park; a meadow and the blank page. Lucky for us, Margolis (as he might put it) gets it down on that blank page before the skittish doe of a thought flees into the woods."

— Alexander Wolf, Senior Writer, *Sports Illustrated*
Big Game, Small World: A Basketball Adventure

In his long and rich career, Gary Margolis has produced a canon that is laudable not only for its monumentality but also, and more importantly, for what I must call its astonishing decency. *Raking the Winter Leaves* is full of elegy, but that elegy is part of its determined, sometimes even gritty celebration.

Wallace Stevens named death the mother of beauty; relatedly, Margolis knows that suffering, his own and others', is the mother of compassion. In "It's You They Come To," a consideration of his equally distinguished career as a member of a college mental health staff, he asks,

Isn't that

what you're here for, too?

To listen to the wheezing

songs inside their chests,

to sing something a mother,

a father might sing,

if only they were here....

Like his awkward and aching patients, we come too, finding in these fine poems the sense, which they roundly justify, that our poet knows where our hearts live, as few others can."

—Sydney Lea, Vermont State Poet
I was Thinking of Beauty

Praise for earlier collections:

from *Fire in the Orchard*

Ralph Waldo Emerson once said that poetry is 'what will and must be spoken,' and in his new book—Gary Margolis speaks in a deceptively quiet but nonetheless urgent voice of what usually goes unspoken, of the spaces between people, the distances we keep, the mortality we bear. Fire in the Orchard is carefully crafted and psychologically astute, a work of emotional attainment, necessary speech.

—Edward Hirsh
The Living Fire: New and Selected Poems

What I treasure about these poems, so diverse in their concerns, is the thread of passionate decency that unifies them. Gary Margolis believes that Godmay be found among the weeds, and that this jangled world can draw us into the numinous if we only stay alert to the ground-level pulsings that can lead us there. His spare recollective voice fiercely and tenderly sings us on our way.

—Ron Powers
Mark Twain: A Life

from *Below the Falls*

Below the Falls is among the handful of recent volumes that has sunk deep into my mind and heart. I love the wit on display hee, a wry and winsome quality as in the opening lines of 'Foreclosure,' where the poet writes: 'I sell my house back to God. The mice can't afford it.' But there is a ferocious, even angry, quality that emerges in these poems, many of which concern the bitter harvest of war. As the writer contemplates the 'dead ready to be taken, baled and stored in the ground's impressionable barn,' he takes us to the center of our complex, often dark, history. In poem after poem, Gary Margolis proves himself in this mature, lucid and humane volume by one of our most accomplished and indispensable poets.

—Jay Parini
Promised Land: Thirteen Books that Changed America

Margolis' generous and humane poems press their worries toward the hopes we might all find ourselves turning to: 'Isn't that what a soul is for, what we can't see?' Finally, inexplicable absence— the disappearance in winter of a young man eventually to have drowned—becomes the certainty of loss, and a local truth resonates with what none of us can see or explain, although we, like the poems themselves, can't help but try: 'Even the dead are guessing they know where they are…The searchers search beyond belief.'

—Lawrence Raab
The History of Forgetting

Below the Falls offers a world in which everything melts away and nothing is lost. Gary Margolis manages in this collection to evoke both the heart's wayward immediacy and its loving tenacity. I feel personally grateful for his way of mapping a path through a long Vermont winter into the sometimes troubled irrepressibility of spring.

—John Elder
Reading the Mountains of Home

from *Seeing the Songs:*
A Poet's Journey to the Shamans in Ecuador

Gary Margolis writes important poems about important subjects, which he understands in emotional and intellectual depth, as *Seeing the Songs*, this fine book, now demonstrates in his lyrical prose.

—Bill McKibben
Eaarth: Making a Life on a Tough, New Planet

Seeing the Songs IS being there. When you enter this incredible book, you enter a world where dreams and reality weave each other and "fact becomes poetry, poetry becomes fact." A brilliant book!

—John Perkins
Confessions of an Economic Hitman

Whether sharing his intense experiences with Otavalo shamans in Ecuador, his journey through craters, playing ball with locals or his adventures in the jungle with the Shuar people, Gary Margolis genuinely shares his experiences as if unashamedly talking to his best friends.

—Ximena Mejia Ph.D, LMHC,
Director of Counseling, Middlebury College

Gary Margolis emerges as a Poet in the Emersonian sense: a Seer whose eyes are opened to the world and whose heart and mind sing back this wisdom in words.

—Rebecca Gould Ph.D.
At Home in Nature:
Modern Homesteading and Spiritual Practice in America

Book design by Kirsty Anderson
Typeset in Bembo Book MT Pro
Cover design by Henry James
Manufactured by Versa Press

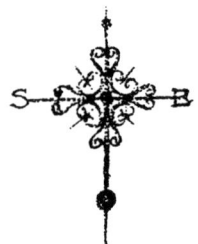